PWE269

P3

REVELATIONS
Glimpses of Reality

REVELATIONS
Glimpses of Reality

Edited by
Ronald S Lello

Foreword by
Sir Alister Hardy FRS

Shepheard-Walwyn (Publishers) Ltd
and Border Television Plc

First published 1985 by
Shepheard-Walwyn (Publishers) Limited
26 Charing Cross Road (Suite 34)
London WC2H ODH

ISBN 0 85683 079 8

British Library Cataloguing in Publication Data

Revelations: glimpses of reality: interviews with
 twelve distinguished personages about their
 spiritual experience.
 1. Experience (Religion)
 I. Lello, Ronald S.
 291.4'2   BL53

ISBN 0-85683-079-8

Typeset by Alacrity Phototypesetters,
Banwell Castle, Weston-super-Mare
Printed and bound in Great Britain by
Billing & Sons Limited, Worcester.

CONTENTS

OUR APPRECIATION TO

Border Television Production Team

Interviewers:

Melvyn Bragg   Eric Robson

Interviewees:

Michael Bentine	P.J. Kavanagh	Doug Scott
Sheila Cassidy	Krishnamurti	Paul Tortelier
Sir Fred Hoyle	Sarah Miles	Sir Laurens van der Post
Yusuf Islam	Iris Murdoch	Kenneth Williams

Producer:

Nick Evans

Channel Four Commissioning Editor:

John Ranelagh

I would especially like to thank Jim Graham whose inspiration led to the creation of this series; Nick Evans for his patient and practical guidance and Sheila Dyett for her considerable help and skill in preparing this manuscript.

Ronald S. Lello
March 1985

FOREWORD

When I am invited to write a Foreword to a book, as a rule I decline, because I think such is unnecessary. This, however, is different. There are a number of things I would like to say about this most important book, so I regard it as a privilege to be allowed to say them here.

First of all I would like to congratulate Border Television on their brilliant conception and great enterprise in putting forward this remarkable programme of twelve interviews on the subject of Revelation. Secondly, I particularly wish to express my admiration and gratitude to Mr. Ronald Lello; his contribution to the series and the preparation of this book has shown immense care.

Am I not exaggerating, some may say, in speaking of this book as being *most* important? I believe not, and I want to say just why I think so; to do this, however, will require quite a little essay which I hope the reader will forgive.

To my mind, the two greatest books on men's relationship to the universe since the publication of Darwin's *Origin of Species* were both published at the turn of the century, and both by American psychologists. One was William James, who gave the Gifford Lectures at Edinburgh in 1901 and published them in his famous book *The Varieties of Religious Experience* in 1902, and the other was Edwin Starbuck, who published *The Psychology of Religion* in 1899. I have put James first because, although he came later, his book is undoubtedly the greater of the two.

One had hoped and expected that these two books would have been followed up excitedly by the intellectual world, but it wasn't so; this was partly due, but not entirely, to the arrival of the psychology of Sigmund Freud, another reason being the shock of the first world war. The only people who really followed James and Starbuck were the social anthropologists who went out to live with the primitive tribes whose religion they were studying: notably Professor Sir Edward Evans-Pritchard (*Nuer Religion*, Oxford, 1956) and Dr. Godfrey Lienhardt (*Divinity and Experience – The Religion of the Dinka*, Oxford 1961). As a result of the work of these anthropologists we know much more about the spiritual experience of primitive people — their revelations — than we do about those of our modern contemporaries in the western world. Evans-Pritchard once told me that he became a Christian through his encounter with the spiritual nature of the Nuers' conception of God; he became a Roman Catholic. There is an interesting parallel here to the experience of Kenneth Williams through the actions of men of another faith.

In discussing the anthropologists I should also mention Emile Durkheim, the great French social anthropologist. I will give two quotations from his book *Elementary Forms of Religious Life* (English translation by J. W. Swain, 1915).

> The believer, who has communicated with his god, is not merely a man who sees new truths of which the un-believer is ignorant; he is a man who is *stronger*. He feels within him more force, either to endure the trials of existence, or to conquer them. It is as though he were raised above the miseries of the world, because he is raised above his condition as a mere man; he believes that he is saved from evil, under whatever form he may conceive this evil. The first article in every creed is the belief in salvation by faith.

Many who have not read Durkheim with sufficient care have thought that his theory of religion is one simply linking it to a *mechanistic* interpretation of the evolution of man as a social animal. Nothing could be further from the truth, as is clearly shown by Durkheim's statement:

> . . . it is necessary to avoid seeing in this theory of religion a simple restatement of historical materialism: that would be misunderstanding our thought to an extreme degree.

I have discussed these authors at some length because I believe this book *Revelations* is in a direct line with the work of James, Starbuck, Evans-Pritchard, Lienhardt and Durkheim. It is an important new step in the development of this line of thought, which establishes the reality of man's relation to what he calls God. It is new in that it reports actual interviews with the people concerned.

I must not discuss the differences between the twelve examples here published, for I do not wish to take the wind out of their sails; they must speak for themselves and come upon the reader with surprise. They come from a great many different walks of life, from a university professor, Fellow of the Royal Society, to a pop star and a comedian. I would, however, like to comment on just one example, for it touches on my own biological field of work.

Regarding Sir Fred Hoyle's contribution, I must say at once that I disagree entirely with his interpretation of the Darwinian theory. I am a staunch Darwinian, or neo-Darwinian, but I am not a materialist. I would agree with him that the influence of the Darwinian theory produced a very materialistic outlook through much of the intellectual world. Darwin, of course, never sought to explain the actual origin of life but only the process by which one form is evolved from another; and it is well to recall the final paragraph of his great book *The Origin of Species*. Darwin wrote thus:

'There is grandeur in this view of life, with its several powers, having been originally breathed by the Creator into a few forms or into one; and that, whilst this planet has gone cycling on according to the fixed law of gravity, from so simple a beginning endless forms most beautiful and most wonderful have been, and are being, evolved.'

There is no doubt that the Darwinian theory gives us an account of the evolution of the physical and chemical nature of living organisms, but it does not deal with the mental side of life. It is also important to realise that whilst Darwin gave his great book the title *The Origin of Species* he was not really dealing with the nature of species formation.

Hoyle, however, is perfectly correct in saying that Darwinian evolution does not take account of the conscious part of life, which I believe, with him, to be far more important than the physical nature of the evolving organisms which contain this element of life. Hoyle talks little about the nature of the revelation he received and its influence upon his life: his frequent references, however, to the happening on the road to Damascus imply that he feels there can be a sudden revelation, or something very important, which influences the whole outlook of the individual and to which he might give the name of God.

I now want to say something that I have never said before, not because I am afraid to say it, but because I might be thought arrogant in putting these views forward. I have to admit that from time to time I feel intellectually ashamed of the modern academic attitude to what one might call the study of the nature of LIFE. I have the greatest admiration for the biochemists and physicists who are telling us so much about the physical nature of the animal body which is the vehicle carrying what we may call the living essence of the organism — the nature of the DNA and the concept of the genetic code. Biology, I believe, is something more. The most important feature about living things is the nature of consciousness. At present it is largely ignored, because one cannot see a method of investigating it; but there can be no doubt that it is there, and not just confined to man. No one who has kept a dog or a horse and has grown really fond of them can doubt that they are conscious beings like ourselves. It was the late Professor Michael Polanyi who showed us the reality of animal consciousness. In his famous Gifford Lectures published as *Personal Knowledge* (1958) he makes a vital distinction by dividing knowledge into two main kinds and by so doing emphasizes that man's mental life is not only in one important and obvious respect radically different from that of his animal ancestry, but is in another more fundamental way much nearer to the animal world than perhaps has ever been thought before, even by the most confirmed evolutionists. His two kinds of knowledge are *explicit knowledge*, that which is formulated in words, maps, mathematical symbols, etc., and *tacit knowledge*, that which is not so formulated, for example the knowledge of what we are in the act of doing or experiencing before we express it in words or symbols. When we go for a country walk by ourselves we gain a knowledge of the scenery through which we are passing and we appreciate its beauty without necessarily describing it to ourselves in words; only later, on getting home, we may give a verbal description of it.

The more primitive forms of human knowledge — those forms of intelligence which man shares with animals — are situated, says Polanyi, behind the barrier of language. Animals have no speech (beyond systems of communication by signs and sounds); the towering superiority of man over the animals is almost entirely due to his development of language. Speech enables man to formulate ideas, to reflect upon them, and communicate them to others. Babies up to eighteen months or so are said to be not much superior to chimpanzees of the same age; only when they learn to speak do they leave the apes far behind. Even adult humans, however, show no distinctly greater intelligence than animals, so long as their minds work unaided by language. 'In the absence of linguistic clues,' says Polanyi, 'man sees things, hears things, feels things, moves about, explores his surroundings and gets to know his way about very much as animals do.'

The coming of language and explicit knowledge altered

the whole course of evolution. By communicating in words, men were able to build up traditions; evolution, instead of being entirely governed by Darwinian selection, became largely a matter of developing traditions. Man is still subject to natural selection by the action of pathogenic organisms or conditions of the environment, but all the time medical science and technological skills are reducing these, so that there is now almost as much difference between man and the animal world as between animals and plants. They are new types of creatures carrying forward the line of evolution.

Polanyi's concepts have been almost entirely neglected by the philosophers of today, yet they are fundamental to our understanding of the nature of life. The revelations which are being discussed in this book of course lie, first of all, in the tacit phase; only later do they become explicit, when people are questioned about the nature of their feelings. So often, particularly in the case of the real mystics, they will tell you that their experience is quite ineffable; and here we see the difficulty in many of the examples given in this book of the drawing out of people's tacit knowledge of what they have experienced.

I remarked earlier that I have often felt ashamed at the lack of attention paid by the academic world to the revelations received by man. It seems extraordinary, to me, why this should be so. There is nothing so emotionally disturbing, or exciting, as the impact of different revelations upon the life of a man. Here, to my mind, is something of great biological significance. There is nothing to equal the emotional disturbance of man by his impact with religion; the only thing that can approach it is that of the jealousies of sex. The wars of religion have always been far more bitter than those fought for economic ends. We have only to look at the appalling clashes between members of different faiths: Sikhs and Hindus, Moslems and Jews, and, alas, in our own country, between Catholics and Protestants. The terrible atrocities committed in the name of religion cannot be equalled by any actions committed in the name of sex. To my mind, it appears that with the coming of explicit knowledge man has entered a new biological phase in which the differences between various types of faith have had tremendous biological significance. R. R. Marret, another of the social anthropologists, has pointed out, just as Durkheim did, that man's religion gives him courage and strength, and lifts him above his normal self. He becomes braver, and the primitive tribes who had this revelation were the more successful. It has, as he says, survival value. It may be, indeed, because of this that man comes to have as passionate a feeling towards his religion as he does in regard to sex.

I must apologise for making my Foreword so much longer than one would expect such a simple introduction to be. I just wanted to stress why I regard this book as of such importance. It is a little gem in the growing field of interest in the study of life. I hope that its readership will be as great as it deserves to be.

Sir Alister Hardy
January, 1985

MICHAEL BENTINE

MICHAEL BENTINE was born in Watford in 1922 and was educated at Eton. His extraordinary career has included such diverse activities as explorer, art critic, journalist and parapsychologist, but he is of course best known as 'Goon' and comedian. One of his own television series, *It's a Square World*, won the Golden Rose of Montrose Critics' Award and his autobiography *The Long Banana Skin* is a best-selling book. He has recently published a new book *Doors to the Mind* in which he develops some of the ideas discussed during this interview.

Interviewed by Eric Robson

What was it like as a small boy living with a constant stream of mediums and magicians coming and going through the house?

There were one or two frightening experiences but then you could have a frightening experience anywhere. It was a very exciting and very interesting period of my life. In fact I preferred being in my own home because I was so shy. When I was finally persuaded to go and visit some friends' homes, I thought how very dull it was because none of the furniture moved on its own!

But wasn't your father trying to involve you in his work?

He thought that if you were looking for truth, surely truth couldn't hurt your family. So why try and separate your family. Surely they should try and share in the general search. He was basically a Christian and he thought of all things like, 'A little child shall lead them' and 'Think as a child and you will enter the Kingdom of Heaven' and all the things that are stated as having been said by the gentle carpenter of Nazareth. When you think about it, that is precisely the route that you take. With a young mind you are dealing with a mind that doesn't suffer from doubt and hasn't got any prejudice, is not politically inclined and is not lying for its own sake. It is a mind that sees very clearly and very quickly.

But what were the sort of things that happened in the family home that convinced you there was substance in what your father was trying to do?

Well firstly, the atmosphere. With a child, atmosphere is everything. You could get a wonderful feeling of power in the room. Nobody has spoken to you about it or tried to convince you that there was power in the room — you felt it. You felt a terrific cold draught up your spine and a lovely feeling, as though there was something awfully good

3

there and you felt very safe and very happy and wonderful
— you'd look round and everybody else was feeling the
same. So you thought to yourself, 'Hello, there's something happening here that's out of the normal.' When the
furniture started moving around you also felt cold. When
this solid piece of Victorian furniture started hopping
around the room with just people putting their fingers on
it, obviously you were experiencing something that was
a harnessing of some form of energy that normally you
didn't see. I mean, you don't usually walk down the street
with tables following you around the place! Equally,
there seemed to be the generation of a feeling of peace with
it.

There were one or two mediums who came. Eddie Part-
ridge was a man who was a very strong psychic medium.
And he had one of those marvellous shops in Dover which
he lived in and he bred his pigeons in the back garden. You
could buy anything from a needle to an anchor and it smelt
of sugar, spice and HP sauce and all sorts of lovely, homely
things: cheese and freshly cooked ham under glass. Eddie
was one of those lovely people with black bands on his arms
to keep his shirt sleeves clean and he always wore a clean
shirt and a celluloid collar. A wonderful, lovely, glowing
little man. He was talking one day and a biscuit salesman
was present and was trying to sell him biscuits. Suddenly
one of the 10 pound weights went whistling through the air
and Eddie said: 'Oh!' — you see, he was very shy of talking
about this sort of thing — and Dad said: 'Oh!' and the
salesman said, 'What the Hell was that?' Eddie said: 'It
might have been a draught.' 'Draught, my elbow!' he said
and picked up his order book like a talisman, held it round
him and ran out of the shop. And I remember Eddie saying
to my father: 'Ah yes, we'll have to sit tonight.' Obviously
it had been some sort of a sign. But there was never any
feeling of a sinister power with Eddie. He was a healer. He

was the type of man who made you feel better as soon as you met.

I was worried about the war like every young person was. I was about 17 when it broke out and 19 when I went into it. I saw some pretty horrific things from then onwards and went through quite a deal of pain. I remember the lazy summer just before the war and Eddie picked up I was worried. He said: 'I want to show you something Michael.' This was about 11 o'clock at night and we'd motored over from Folkestone. As we drove out into the country, Eddie said, 'Stop here!' We walked into the wood and all you could hear was the swishing of our legs as we went through the ferns. We came to the centre of the wood, which was very dense, and came across a clearing. Eddie turned and I could see him smiling in the moonlight. He made one sound, very softly. It was half-way between a whistle and a word. And every bird, every beast, every rabbit, every vole, every little creature of the woods and, I think the insects as well, answered him. One of the most moving things I think I've ever experienced in my life. He was so close to nature, that she instantly knew him and recognised him for what he was. And it is that which I would try and raise in a child. The awareness of nature is what I've always had, I've been very lucky.

But in later years I know you had a more harrowing vision during the days when you were working with RAF air crew during the Second World War.

Well you see, you were so much in rapport with them that you knew their mental condition, their psychological condition. I was a frustrated penguin, I wanted to fly. I got part of the way through my training when they gave me an injection which nearly killed me. It killed one person, paralysed another and put me flat on my back for six months. It actually blinded me for a time. So I couldn't fly anymore. But all I wanted to do was to be with air crew because I could be with aircraft. My father designed aeroplanes. I only wanted to fly aeroplanes. My family ran an airline in Peru. So the air to me was my *raison d'etre*.

The great link with all air crew was that they wanted to fly. But because aircraft were not safe, it was a terrible death. I mean I had friends whom I just couldn't release from the fuselage in which they were trapped. They were caught and you watched them burn. There was all that horror to see. But also there was the feeling of flight and I flew every time I could. I was very close to air crew and they were very close to me and they trusted me. I knew exactly what their mental condition was. If I saw a look come over their face, I knew they were going to die. Not that they would be shot down or that they would be taken prisoner or they'd parachute safely. 'That man would die that night on that flight'.

The awful thing was, one was never wrong. One was picking up something, a negative force of energy from that man. He wasn't fit to fly that night, that's what it's all about. I tried once going to the Medical Officer and saying, 'Look that man, that man and that man, are not fit to fly tonight.' He said, 'There's nothing I can do about it, there's no outward sign that they are unfit.' But to me there was and that was the night that they 'bought it'.

But what exactly was it that you saw in the faces of those airmen that you knew were going to their deaths?

They looked as though they were dead. Virtually they had the death's head. You saw death in their face. And it happened again and again and again. It was one hundred percent accurate, not ninety percent or eighty percent, it was a hundred percent accurate. And it was really getting to me.

It wasn't the fear or the emotion of the moment?

No! Oh no, no! When you're 21 years old you don't have that amount of emotion in you: you're carried along by the expertise of your training, which was very intense indeed, and the comradeship and the rapport that you have with the air crew. You're a total professional or you don't live, it's that simple.

Did you talk to your mates in the barracks about this?

No I didn't. I learnt when I was a small boy not to talk about these things, because I usually got beaten up if I did talk about them. It was the crazy, the looney, the idiot, the Peruvian, the dago, the whole bit. So I just kept quiet about this side of it.

But when you were having an experience like that – did you feel that someone out there was trying to communicate something through you?

No, no! It's like contacting a fund of information. You could say that the experience I was having was a horrible experience, an outward sign or symbol of the fact that the man was in such a psychological state that he wasn't safe to fly. That's really what we are talking about. But I didn't see a large figure beside me with wings on saying, 'Look at that man, he has a death's head.' There was none of that. It was a sudden conviction that that man would die.

   I went to the padre and I said to him, 'I've had enough of this' and I explained what had happened. He wasn't in the least bit surprised. He said, 'Oh, you're not the first one to come here. I had it in the First World War.' When he was a youngster, before he was a padre, he'd been in the Guards or something like that, fighting in the trenches. And he said he'd had the same experience — that anybody could know it who had a close rapport in this tremendous effort of war, which is a complete effort of mind and body and will. All your antennae are out. He said as Goethe said: 'Coming events cast their shadows before them' and that was really what I was seeing.

So it might be picking up the vibrations of someone standing next to you in the briefing room?

No, no. It's much stronger than that. It wasn't a question of 'Oh, he might die tonight'. It was, 'He will die tonight, he won't and he won't, but he will and he will' — just like that!

When you were having experiences as powerful and as moving for you as that, did you ever think that you were actually losing your reason?

No, why should I? I see people who say, 'Now let us reason this out. We're going to spend seven billion pounds on this new weapon which we will never use because it's so devastating that we can't use it.' Is that reason? But it's said by a reasonable man who has been elected by the people to take a reasonable decision. Yet to me that's madness! What I saw was madness but I often wonder if it isn't the other way round. What one person will call reason another person will call madness. What one person will call a freedom fighter another person will call a terrorist. It's a comparative thing.

No, I didn't think I was going mad because the point was that it was happening every time. It was only another manifestation of what I'd been taught. Open my mind and scan and pick up the truth. We were looking at the truth and that was the truth. That night that man would die. That was the truth we were picking up.

You've been in the presence of images of real evil. I know you visited Belsen just a few hours after the camp was liberated. How did your open-minded approach respond to those images?

Well I shut off immediately and so did everybody else there. You just shut your mind to it and got on with what you had to do. I didn't have to do it, it wasn't my particular job, it's just that everybody flocked to help. I mean there were these people walking around like something out of Dante's Inferno. You had to help them, you had to do something. The stench was unbelievable. If you had opened your mind it would have blown it instantly.

You have also experienced considerable personal tragedy. Can you describe the circumstances surrounding your son's death?

Well, I warned him that this was going to happen. I very seldom warn my children about anything. I don't interfere with my children's lives. We were all laughing in the nursery; my wife and myself and my son. And suddenly this laughing face turned into the same death's head that I'd seen with air crew. And I knew then that he was going to die or that there was a strong likelihood of him dying. And then secondly, I saw a light plane which seemed to go up in the air and then crash. It was so clear and so shocking that I'd blurted out what I'd seen and then I took him next door, because my wife was naturally very upset and so was he. I told him what I'd seen. And I said, 'You must warn your friend that if you two fly together for some reason, it will be a matter of two lifelines. And if those cross, that's it! He can be the best pilot and he still won't be able to fly it.' Of course that's what happened. It took the air accident branch a long time to prove it but they did prove it.

I felt my son come to me in my garden within 48 hours of him actually passing. I remember it very clearly. He said, 'I'm terribly sorry daddy. It wasn't Andy's fault. The bloody machine went wrong in the air!' Not the most spiritual message that has ever passed from son to father! Nevertheless it took two years to prove it and that was exactly the result of the investigation; the machine had gone wrong in the air.

How would you respond to sceptics, Michael, who would say that

*is simply because you wanted to have another contact with your
son?*

Well, do tell me what qualifications these splendid sceptics
have. Presumably they've known me for fifty-two years so
they would know whether I was self-deluded or not. It's
amazing how people can come up and say: 'I've never met
you in my life before but from my considered omniscient
point of view, as a god-like being, I can tell you now you're
totally self-deluded. I don't know you, I've never met you
but I know, by the fact that I'm omniscient.' There are so
many people like that but I know what I experienced. If it
was self-delusion, it was odd that the whole of the air
accident branch were also self-deluded for two years.

There are so many people that come up and say: 'Why
don't you admit your son is dead?' And I always say, 'O.K.
Does that give you a kick. Does that make you feel better?
Now go away.' I say it very rudely. And I'm not a rude man
by nature. I find there are so many omniscient geniuses who
know it all. I'll tell you my own point is I know nothing. I
just have a very simple conviction based on fifty-two years
of conscious experience. That's what I base my faith on.

*You said that your conviction was unshakable and yet you've had
an inordinate amount of suffering in your life: your son's been
killed, your daughter died of cancer and another daughter had
cancer, did none of that shake your conviction in the force of good?*

What on earth has cancer got to do with goodness? What
has crashing an aeroplane got to do with goodness? Goodness is positive thinking. We're talking about accidents and
of cells going mad.

*So you're talking about a God, a Supreme Being who is directing
things?*

I cannot conceive of a God like that. That's a human idea of

God. To me God is everything. I'm a very keen amateur astronomer, very inept but very keen, and I have instruments that will look deep into space and I keep seeing miracles every time I look out. You talk about revelations. Look through a very powerful telescope some night and you'll have so many revelations, your mind will start tumbling. You'll be looking into the face of God, or at least, part of the face of God.

I've always had a child's view of God. A very simple view of God. God's everywhere. The thing that we're standing on is God. It's a miracle. The thing that we're standing on, we are actually made of! The ambient atmosphere around us we're ingesting, it's giving us life. When we die we go back into the soil, whether we're in the form of ash or in the form of a body. We regenerate into another form of life. You're looking at a constant miracle. That's what's so exciting about life.

Do you believe that anyone could open their minds sufficiently to experience the sort of array of images that you've talked to us about?

Every child can do it and every child does it. A child has infinite capacity. I don't believe that William Golding is right in *The Lord of the Flies* — put a group of children together and you will see evil — because at the end of the war I saw groups of children, the eldest might be twelve and the youngest would be a baby in arms; if they were that evil, why carry the baby in arms? And there'd be boys and girls maybe fifty of them, running wild. They'd steal anything to live and there was a leader of the pack and there was the rest of the pack. But the feeling of the pack was goodness. You just gave them everything you'd got except your weapons. You didn't give them side arms. I saw all that happen and nobody can turn round and say to me, 'You don't know what you're talking about because you haven't seen the face of horror.' I've seen the face of horror and I still believe that there is a transcendental, positive light in man and that is the only thing that's going to keep him going even though at the moment it looks very much like he is surrounded by darkness, doesn't it?

Michael Bentine, thank you very much.

DR. SHEILA CASSIDY

SHEILA CASSIDY was born in Cranwell, Lincolnshire in 1937. She graduated as a doctor of medicine in 1963 and in 1971 went to Chile where she continued to practice. In 1975 she was arrested and brutally tortured by the Chilean secret police. The incident caused a major diplomatic rift in Britain's relations with Chile and her return to England was marked by extensive publicity. She subsequently spent some time in a monastic discipline before deciding to devote herself to working with the terminally ill. She is actively involved in preaching, lecturing and broadcasting on radio and television.

Interviewed by Eric Robson

About three years after you came back from Chile you wrote: 'At the time our sense of God's presence was largely obscured by the weight of this cross. It was only with the passage of time that I was able to appreciate the quality of revelation in what had happened to me'. What was the quality of revelation that you experienced at that time?

I'd say the most important thing about that experience was that I came away with a deep gut level knowledge that nothing could separate me or others from the love of God. I remember saying to the Consul the first time I saw him, 'Tell my family that Romans VIII is true! "Neither death, nor life, principalities or powers, can separate us from the love of Christ".' It was knowing that at gut level.

Have you always had a strong religious foundation?

No — it waxed and waned. I was a quiet little girl. I was a pretty average sort of Catholic and then the religious thing came over me like a tidal wave when I was a teenager.

What was the moment when your belief became altogether more profound?

There wasn't a particular moment. It was sometime during my last year at school and I think that I was somehow influenced by the nuns who taught me. Not that they said anything pious but that I liked them as people and could communicate with them as people. I began to think, these people are good, I wonder what makes them tick and I found that it was God that makes them tick. And somehow, during that year, I had this sensation of being singled out, called by God and I didn't like it. It wasn't like the Joan of Arc voices. It was interior knowledge. I certainly have never had any experience of God speaking in words. It's more a knowledge from within. It's a knowledge.

How did you come to that conclusion? Why didn't you simply

15

believe you'd thought of the idea of becoming more religious or involving yourself more with the Church?

No, it's not like that: I might for example think I ought to go and work in El Salvador or go and work in Belfast. That would be a thing weighed up. But the other was just a knowing without doubt. It wasn't a thing arrived at through the emotions or through the will.

You said you were terrified or frightened of it.

Yes, and also I was angry because when I was a little girl I could draw and I wanted to be a dress designer. And when I was fifteen, I fell in love with the family doctor and I read a lot of A.J. Cronin. I became very idealistic and suddenly decided to do medicine. I remember saying to my father, 'If only I was a man I could do medicine'. And he who was a very ambitious man said, 'Ah, my darling, but you know women can be doctors.' From that moment on I wanted to be a doctor.

And then suddenly there was God on the scene saying, 'I want you to do something different'.

The way I understood it then was that I thought this meant giving up medicine, and I thought it meant giving up marriage. It seemed to be a destructive thing, wrecking my career and wrecking my chances of marriage.

After that initial reaction, did you find that this gentle revelation, that you had, gave you additional personal strength?

It wasn't gentle nor was it the instantaneous road to Damascus but it threw me into great confusion. Yet I think it probably gave me strength as a school child because I was quite a conservative sort of child and actually I kept it from my parents. I went and found a priest. I went on a long journey into the city to this monastery and sought out a priest although I'd never ever spoken to a priest before. So it gave me strength in that way, it gave me power to my elbow.

Can I take you on now to those events that happened to you in Chile almost ten years ago? How well prepared were you to be able to cope with what in anybody's terms was a horrifying experience? Did you find that your religious belief of earlier years gave you the strength to be able to cope with it?

Although I had had a fairly marked conversion experience, I had in fact lapsed. I hadn't gone to Church or prayed at all for nearly ten years and then I came back to the practise of my faith with a fair vengeance. I went back to being the sort of person who went to Mass every day — I prayed all the time. I used to go and spend whole days in prayer at a local monastery. So these experiences in Chile came to me at a time when I was on a very firm praying basis, as it were.

So when you were in the car on the way to that interrogation centre, whilst you were blindfolded in that room full of men who you knew were going to interrogate you, probably brutally, were you certain that God was with you?

I was certain. I didn't know at that stage that they were going to abuse me. When they started to take off my clothes, I was completely incredulous because I'd always thought that I had a measure of protection, I was English and I was the Air Vice-Marshall's daughter. I had thought I might be killed in crossfire but I never thought I'd be done over in that way. But while it was happening I did have some kind of sense of the presence of God which never left me.

You were certain. Could you feel His presence?

In a very non-comforting sort of way. If you could imagine a situation where somebody you knew was actually a bystander at something horrible happening to you, not intervening, knowing they were there but not achieving any comfort from the fact that that person was there.

Why wasn't your God intervening?

I've no idea why God wasn't intervening. History shows that God doesn't intervene in a lot of things. There's nothing special about me! This is one of the things that I care about because I think that Christians, who think that they have a special share of God's power to sweep in and heal their problems, are kidding themselves.

You have said that you prayed for the men who were torturing you. Yet you felt certain that you were going to be raped by these men. How is it to feel that fear and yet feel that amount of pity, even to the extent of praying for them?

The two things were separated in time. At the time of the interrogation and the fear of rape, I was just surviving minute by minute and being absolutely terrified and not feeling any emotion for the people. The time when I prayed for them and the time when I was sorry for them was a much more reflective period when I was in solitary confinement. I had three weeks to do nothing else but think and pray. So it was separated in time and space.

Do you have any idea why the bitterness that human beings like myself would certainly have felt, didn't arise in you?

I honestly don't know except that I would understand that as a gift from God. I mean, I certainly don't think it's anything to do with me or any virtue of mine. I think it was a gift. I've always thought of it as a gift even at the time when I realised I wasn't bitter. I thought, 'Golly, I should be bitter' and I knew I wasn't.

Did you ever lose your faith? Did you not at any time feel 'a God that can allow this to happen to me is a pretty awful God'?

No, it wasn't like that. The curious thing was that all that time that it was happening, I knew that God loved me. Don't ask me how, but after the torture I was more and more convinced of a loving God who knew and loved me personally.

You wrote a very moving phrase about the 'Cross being too close'. Can you explain to me what you meant by that?

When I wrote that I was talking about the actual moment of torture, it was a very curious clinical thing like God being present in an operating theatre. I think that one can often only discern the hand of God or the Cross from a distance. For example, if I put my hand out I can see it clearly. If I bring it close to my face then it's obliterated and I think that in great mental or physical suffering, God is obscured because if there was a deep sense of God at the actual moment, the suffering wouldn't be so great. It's only in retrospect, in hindsight that one can discern God in history or in events.

Many people have been driven mad by that sort of psychological torture. Was turning to God a way of keeping you sane?

I think it may have kept me sane but it certainly wasn't a deliberate manoeuvre. There were deliberate manoeuvres that I did to keep myself sane. Walking up and down the cell, making lists of people, that sort of thing. But I don't think I used God as a crutch in that way to survive.

There are cynics who might argue that to take belief in God in the way we've been talking about, is rather a cop out or a crutch; a way of avoiding coming to terms with the real issue which is that human beings are doing nasty things to each other.

I just find that funny. Last year I gave fifty-two lectures of which I would say half were human rights lectures designed to break down the barriers of stupidity and ignorance about

torture and injustice — if that's crawling back into the
bunker, God knows, I'd like another bunker!

I suppose it could be, if it is a crutch which drags me out
of bed to pray every day when I would very much rather lie
there and sleep or listen to the radio. It has a very powerful
effect in terms of fidelity. Believe me, I get very little kick
from praying. The vast amount of my prayer is, in fact,
what is known in the trade as 'dry'. It means that I get no
comfort, no consolation and no sense of the presence of God
whilst I'm doing it.

*It is difficult to ask you this but at the end of your ordeal, at the
end of many hours of torture, you gave the names of the nuns and
priests who had brought the wounded man to you for help. Do
you think God has forgiven you for betraying them?*

I don't think God ever blamed me for that because I was
subjected to such very, very severe pain which I wasn't
capable of resisting. It took a long time for me to forgive
myself but, in retrospect, I don't think I needed forgiveness
by God for that.

*What has the long-term effect of those events been? And your
awakening – re-awakening of your knowledge of God?*

I suppose one of the long-term effects of being tortured in
that way is that I know torture is for real, and it has given me
an on-going sense of obligation towards the oppressed and
particularly towards the tortured. That drives me — and I
think that's the right word — to lecture and make appeals on
behalf of the imprisoned. The whole thing of handing over
to God again is an on-going way of living. My life is lived
out, I hope, in the service of God, in a deliberate day to day
way of trying to serve God through man.

If that's taken as the first thing, everything else follows. It
means that in a very real sense I don't care what happens to
me, I don't care if I die today or if I live to be eighty. I just

don't give a fig what happens to me so long as I do what God wants.

Since Chile you were moved by a message of God, to go into a convent but it didn't work out.

I decided that I had misinterpreted the message. I come of a generation of Catholics where the religious life was seen as the highest possible way of serving God. The Church no longer necessarily thinks like that. Some people are called to religious life, some people to marriage. I see my calling as being in the service of God with everything I've got but not as a nun.

I spent a year and a half in a convent as a novice and they threw me out. God knows I tried, nobody could have tried harder. I lay on my face on the floor in that chapel and cried. But I was literally a novice in a convent for a year and a half and the way I interpret it is, that I still feel called to the service of God, but I now realise that I am not called to be a nun. I don't have any sense of rejection of that calling, merely one of pursuing it.

It's quite something to go into a convent at the age of forty-four or whatever it was. It was quite hard, one of the hardest things I've done; much harder than prison. I was actually terribly unhappy and I was very lonely. I was just very lonely and caged.

So you've carried on with your medical work. You work with the terminally ill. Can you give them a better understanding of their own suffering?

I can have compassion with them. I can have understanding with them because they are trapped. I think it's the sense of having no way out that I can share with them. Very often people want to pray but they feel they can't, and so I am able to tell people that it's very, very difficult to pray when they are in terrible pain. For example in the hospice we have a wooden cross that we give people and they grip that and I say, 'You may not have the words to pray but just grip, hang on, if you like, pray with your hands.' It's a matter of praying with the will rather than with the emotions. There's no emotion left for pious thoughts about God when you're in terrible pain. It's a thing of the will.

Is it not difficult for those people – surely they are bound to say if God is so loving and benign why has he given me cancer?

I think you're projecting your problems onto them! Some of them do have this difficulty but a lot of people don't. Many people already come to me with their faith deeper. Some people come with no faith and we are able to help them. Some people don't talk about it at all. People vary. But sometimes we say we know what people must be thinking and we are not always right.

Sheila Cassidy, thank you very much.

SIR FRED HOYLE

SIR FRED HOYLE, F.R.S., scientist and astronomer, was born in 1915 in the North of England. From an early age he questioned the basic propositions of scientific theory and he has subsequently established a reputation for brilliant and radical thought. His association with the 'steady state' theory of the universe brought him to the public eye and as this interview indicates, he has continued to develop his thinking about the meaning of existence in the finest scientific tradition. His book *The Intelligent Universe* is the most recent of some 47 scientific works and science fiction novels. He has also written a play and a libretto *The Alchemy of Love*. He now lives in the Lake District where he continues his work.

Interviewed by Melvyn Bragg

Why did you come to the conclusion that Darwinism was wrong?

There is a misapprehension about what Darwinism or the theory of biological evolution really amounts to. The idea in many people's minds is that it's natural selection. It simply says that the varieties and forms which are best fitted to survive will survive. But it does absolutely nothing for evolution. If you had a lorry load of potatoes you could select them for their sizes, shapes and smoothness but you wouldn't be able to convert them into a lorry load of tomatoes which is the sort of thing involved in the idea of evolution.

Darwin tries to explain why things develop variations in a way which every biologist today would agree is wrong. In the early years of this century, biologists thought that the variations arise for no particular reason. But can you arrive at anything as complex as life by random effects? The real question is where do the variations come from?

Did you also find it in some ways morally objectionable?

It did dawn on me as I began to think that, if you can only get from a worse form to a better form with the worst form having to become extinct, this can create a justification for all manner of actions which have a moral quality to them. Can you say it doesn't matter how you treat animals because they're inferior forms? Once you realise that we're all part of a similar system, all part of an evolving system and that everything is wonderfully complex down to the simplest forms, then you begin to have a different moral outlook on the question. I now see animals as being as important as ourselves.

Why do you think that your view of Darwinism has been so heavily attacked?

I think it's a matter of education. For instance in music,

there's a correct way to play a scale on a piano and an incorrect way to do it. In these things, education is splendid. But once it comes to a question of beliefs where nobody can be certain, education can become very pernicious. It causes people to accept beliefs at a time when they're not in a position to argue with the people who are teaching them. It becomes an act of faith. Darwinism is very much in this area. Students in biology learn it as an act of faith.

Experience shows that if acts of faith — things you don't have good reason for but you believe in because you've been told to do so — are contradicted, people get mad. It arouses the emotions and people become angry. Darwinism is in the category where people are more or less forced by the educational process to believe it. Yet it doesn't explain the crucial question of where the variations come from.

You mean variations among the species?

Yes. For instance, if I look at the fossil record, the striking thing is that there are no connections at all between the various types of mammals, the various orders of wildlife — biological orders and so on. There are no connections established in the fossil record at all at the higher levels of plants and insects. And then you can get the vertibrates, fishes, birds, mammals — all these broad divisions of living forms and again, there's no connection.

Now people who defend Darwin will say the fossil record is not complete; there are always bits missing. That's true, but by now we have a veritable army of geologists in the field; universities train them in great numbers and, because of the development of the oil business, they're swarming all over the earth looking for oil, and everything has been looked at pretty tightly. You begin to worry a litle if half of the important connections are missing. The real point is, that all of them are missing! When for instance a reptile changes into a mammal, as it is supposed to do, it's a crisis. It happened, if it happened at all, as a major upheaval and all the connections, if they ever existed, have to be enormous upheavals which are not explained by that kind of theory.

What is your explanation?

What happens, I feel, is that the basic information we have has come from outside the earth. You have conglomerates of this information — the biologists call them genes — existing at any time and natural selection operates on these conglomerates. We call a conglomerate a spider or a human being. It operates and directs things just as it's supposed to do, but from time to time the conglomerate changes. I think we are sampling stuff coming from outside all the time. When something happens that really changes the conglomerate decisively, then you get these great jumps and it happens so quickly and so decisively that the geologists just can't pick it up.

Do you have views of this from a moral point of view as well?

Yes, from a moral and social point of view Darwinism fitted the sociology of the day. There's a certain correspondence between his ideas and the way industrial society was changing that appealed to many people. But on the moral side, if you think that you improve by the extinction of other creatures, it becomes a moral justification for making other species extinct.

Some day I would really like to look into it historically, that all of the trouble we've suffered over the last hundred years, is very closely connected with the spreading of this kind of philosophy. I think the bad social history of the last hundred years stems very directly from what we call the Darwinian theory.

How does your rejection of the Big Bang Theory of the universe link in with what you've arrived at in the intelligent universe?

I believe life did not start on the earth: therefore it had to start somewhere else. It means that the universe has to be right to produce life. And life is much the most complicated thing we know anything about. In my view the universe has to have a nature that will provide for us to be here, for life to exist. And once you say that, you can see straight away that the Big Bang Theory can't be right because it is too tight; everything's over in a flash; there's no way it can develop this marvellous order that we see in living systems.

In your book this concept leads to an intelligent universe – can you describe how that intelligence relates to your idea of the formation, or the existence of the universe?

Intelligence is something that can change the way the world behaves by its own thinking — just as a human farmer can change what can happen in his fields and we can change the buildings and so forth. When we look at stars and galaxies, there is evidence that the way things are has been deliberately ordered. There are too many aspects of our physical existence that would otherwise be coincidental — the proportions of carbon and oxygen that exist on an astronomical scale are right for living creatures. There are all sorts of clever little tricks of that kind which the Americans would call a 'Fix'. It looks like a 'Fix'. Some guide, some influence has been at work, just as we're at work.

But does denying the Big Bang Theory mean that you oppose the idea that there was a start and a beginning?

Yes, absolutely, but I'm not going to argue whether there was a beginning or not because then we're into philosophy. I'm saying, if there is a beginning, it's all enormously more remote. There's not room, there's not time for anything to happen in the Big Bang.

From the knowledge we have of the universe, I think I have to admit that we can see the universe has evolved from some previous condition. What the Big Bangites say is it evolved from an origin when the universe was very different from the way it is now — fantastically hot and fantastically dense and things like that — but you have to realise that this hot, early universe is a concept of minds. It is a mass of mathematical symbols. It's not ovulations in the way that stars and galaxies are ovulations. The question is how do you connect this world of the human brain with what is really fact in the world?

The Big Bang Theory is something which seeks to connect the world as we observe it with what happened before. And if you go back in time you eventually wind up with nothing and the step from nothing to something is what people call the Big Bang. Why I reject it is that it doesn't lead to a connection between the early stages and what we observe today. So that what you have now is a sort of mathematical structure in people's heads — symbols chasing symbols on paper. That's all conjectural.

If you take the standard Big Bang that's the way it is. The psychology of the scientist is very much like the psychology of the religious fundamentalist. He says he can't understand how man could have come about, therefore man must have been created in some way. And the scientist says he can't understand where matter came from therefore it must have been created in the Big Bang.

I have never liked that: I've always worked with a system of mathematics that permits matter to be created. And the good thing now, after going for thirty years with the high grade physicists telling me that it has to be nonsense, is that today we know it can be done.

What is the old Steady State Theory?

It was a situation where we had matter created and this led

to a particular form of the expansion of the universe and allowed one to have a fairly firm platform on which to build for the formation of galaxies and stars. The Steady State provided a firm backdrop against which events could work out. Whereas the Big Bang is like trying to build a large building on quicksands.

What is the place of the creative force or the intelligence in the Steady State system?

It is really a system of mathematics. If you say this particular system of mathematics is true, then such and such has to follow. If you ask what made this system of mathematics true, then you get into what I call 'the Fix'.

In other words there is a guiding intelligence which has ordered something?

Yes, that's right. My concept of the universal intelligence is not as deep rooted as that of a Christian or the Hebrew because they regard their intelligence as all powerful. That leads to the contradiction that an all powerful intelligence would have to be rather peculiar to create a world with such horrible aspects as we find in the actual. In my world it is something where continuing intelligence within the universe is trying to make the best of the situation — just as to a certain degree we humans try to make the best of the world around us.

In a somewhat similar way I think that the intelligence in the universe is trying to cope with something but can't give perfect solutions. So what does it do? It produces a whole system of genetic components which are spread everywhere. And wherever there's a little place like the earth, these things shower on to it and gradually, through the process we call evolution, they begin to produce plants and animals and eventually, a small intelligence like ourselves. We're probably quite a small reflection of the intelligence

that produced us. You might say we are the local repre-
sentative of a larger scale intelligence and, in that sense, to
some extent it does agree with what the formal religions
say.

Now, where is it going? I have a sort of in-built feeling, a
sort of emotion if you like, that it isn't just aimless: that if
these components, these aggregates of components can
reach a certain level, then there is something important to be
done. I also have a feeling that we're getting to the stage
where that objective is not too far away.

*And you see us as 'custodians'? We are something through which
something else is moving?*

That's right. We are reflecting the original process and, in a
small way, we are the original process.

You see this in those few individuals that we call geniuses
—Shakespeare, Mozart. And these chaps are the precursors,
the indicators along the path. The religious people have got
it with St Paul on the road to Damascus. The sudden
light — it's just like that in science. There is a turning point.

*Did you have a moment where the idea of this progression
occurred to you as a probability and you wanted to be convinced by
it?*

Yes. We measured, together with two colleagues, the
properties of actual micro organisms in the laboratory and
we knew that if this whole line of thinking was to be right
the tiny particles in space had to have a very decisive
property. So then we went to the telescope and looked. And
that to me was the moment on the road to Damascus.

What was it telling you? Can you be specific?

It was what we call a 'thumb print', an infra-red thumb
print. If the particles in space have the characteristics of
living material, they have to have this thumb print, a certain

characteristic absorbtion pattern of heat rays. It has to absorb heat rays in a certain way. We had discovered that every sample of living material we examined in the laboratory had this property and nothing else that we found had. And then we looked into the universe and there it was!

You've talked about there being blinding revelation for scientists as well as for religious people.

I've always been impressed by a remark of Einstein's where I think he summed up the whole scientific philosophy when he said, 'God may be subtle but he's not malicious.' It's just a feeling within yourself, it's a light on the road to Damascus.

We knew that the properties of the particles in space had to have this thumb print that living systems have. It happened that the big telescope in Australia had just been fitted with instruments that were well suited to testing this point and two astronomers were already seeking to do similar kinds of observations, so we had to wait about three months. Then the chap came back from Australia. He had the results in his bag and 'phoned to say, 'I've got to sleep for two days' and then darn it all, he sent them through the post! So we had to wait for the post until my colleague got them. He telephoned me immediately without working them out, and gave me the information — long tables of numbers on which we both set to work. It took us about two hours on the 'phone together and we were very excited because the check was marvellous. It proved to me that either the universe was malicious, that we're being deliberately led in the wrong direction, or that life has this universal property and we are a component in a large scale system.

If we go back to the road to Damascus, St. Paul had been putting conditionals on his thinking and suddenly they were removed. This is why it is an intensely personal experience. It can only happen if one has gone through a sort of crisis either of moral, mathematical or scientific thinking.

In the case of science it can be proved, you can convince people by evidence, can't you?

The thing which convinces people most is if you make a prediction which turns out to be true. It really is very similar to moral issues and religious issues. I think everybody has to travel the road to Damascus.

What actually happens is that when enough people have gone through the crisis point themselves and form a sort of caucus opinion, they begin to teach this to their students who in turn begin to learn a different point of view as a matter of faith and belief. It means that whenever any real shift has to come, it comes from a few people to begin with then more and more, until eventually it gets on to the lecture rostrum in schools. From then on everybody believes it.

You've been talking about intelligence working its way through and us being custodians of intelligence which operates on the grandest circuit as well as on local circuits. Looking around the world as it exists at this moment in 1984, the intelligence seems to be failing.

I have a strong feeling that when you get to a certain level of technology not much time will be left before one will wipe oneself out unless these other ideas — which might be called religious — become fixed. In other words, the slice of time left to us is very short. Unless people get away from the prejudice of three thousand years ago, which is the formal religion or from the scientist with no religion, another planet will have failed. However, there are plenty of planets and a few get through although each one has only a small slice of time.

You're right, the world does not look good. We've reached the stage where we can destroy ourselves a hundred times over in half an hour and that's a pretty grim possibility. Unless people sort themselves out, I don't think there is much time ahead.

I think one of the things people who are pro-Darwin feel, is that he destroyed religion. Although many things that I've said are not favourable to religion in detail, this business of a religious instinct, the sanctity of the truth and so on, are signposts that will prevent our self-destruction.

Sir Fred, thank you very much.

YUSUF ISLAM

YUSUF ISLAM known to millions as Cat Stevens, was born in London in 1948. His Greek family gave him a familiarity with the music of their culture at an early age. His rapid rise to fame as a popular musician brought with it the notoriety which the Press associates with the 'pop' culture. In 1968 he fell victim to a serious respiratory illness and he spent several months in hospital. He returned in 1970 to compose and sing a run of memorable songs including the much loved, 'Morning Has Broken'. He first encountered the Islamic faith in 1975 and has for many years practised as a devout Muslim. He is the Director of the Islamic Circle and a Trustee of the Islamia Primary School.

Interviewed by Eric Robson

It's become rather a cliché of the gossip columns that the glamour of the pop star's life is actually hell if you're living it?

The music busines is connected quite a lot with hell I should think. But I wouldn't say it's all like that. There is a good side to it providing you can see it for what it is.

As a child at least one member of your family was Greek Orthodox – were you drawn to any particular religion?

I received a basic Christian upbringing. I didn't really question that because you take it for granted that your parents know better than you. As I grew up in that atmosphere there did seem to be a dichotomy or separation between what seems to be the spiritual ideal and the actual material life, the things going on around me. I suppose because of the attraction of the life of the world and because the religious life seemed kind of difficult and not quite for me, I went naturally into the life of the world. I was brought up in the West End of London so I think that had something to do with me going into show business.

But in the late Sixties it seemed that scarcely a week went by without some pop star or other heading for the hills in India or Nepal to sit at the feet of a Guru. Were you ever tempted to take that path?

Yes, in fact, that was part of my journey. I think I'd just had a brief career in the beginning with my early songs and then I'd contracted tuberculosis around 1969. That made me think more seriously about life. I started studying meditation. In a way I'd lost my faith in Christianity, I suppose because I felt that it was too linked with the system and I wanted to break away from the system. I believed in God — but not through any particular dogma or doctrine.

What do you mean 'linked with the system'?

It seemed to me that the Christian faith had a kind of a

37

hierarchy built in with it. I wanted something more natural, perhaps more spiritual, which I didn't find in the Church.

When you were struck down with TB, did you at any time feel that this was a sort of divine retribution? I mean the typical headline about Cat Stevens had been, 'Cat Stevens the man with the fast ladies and fast cars'.

I thought that was nature working its way out. But, of course, there was also the other thought that I had somehow to find out what this nature is and what it wants from me. I still believed deeply in God but I didn't know exactly how to connect or what exactly God wanted from me.

And, during this time of spiritual quest, you tried a number of things. You didn't immediately come to Islam?

I tried meditation. I was a vegetarian. I believed, of course, with many of my generation, in peace and love but I had no idea of the practical ways of achieving it. I had also become interested in Zen and in astrology. You go through all these phases. I didn't think there was any particular religion which seemed to have the universal answer or meaning. I didn't think there was such a faith, I thought perhaps I'd have to make up my own religion if you like.

Can you tell us how you knew that Islam was the way forward for you?

I was about twenty-seven at that time and I'd been searching without actually finding the peace for which I was looking. Then I was given a copy of the Qur'an and that's really how I began to embrace Islam. It was a gift from my elder brother, David. When I started to read the Qur'an it struck me that this was like no other book I'd ever come across. The words seemed to be so straightforward and spoke with such authority. It didn't seem as if any human being had written this book.

Was there one sentence in the Qur'an that unlocked the secret for you?

Well, I think if you take the Qur'an as a whole, it could just have happened like that with one sentence. It was a gradual awakening to the fact that the more I read it, the more I realised there was no contradiction, whereas all other books I knew had to have something wrong with them. There was something about this book that didn't show any signs of imperfection.

The thing that struck me was the testimony in the Qur'an; the constant testimony to the fact that there is only one God. And that gave me the message that I was looking for. This was something which I felt had to be accepted by everyone because everyone by nature, believes in some higher power, some controlling force. Many names are given but essentially it comes down to this; there has to be only one for all! That led to changing my whole view of life. It naturally brings you to understand that people are equal because we're all created by the same God; we're all servants of the same Lord. It gives you a kind of feeling that there is unity, purpose and bond between human beings and that's what I found to be the most impressive aspect of the Qur'an.

If I can quote a very small chapter. This is called the Chapter of Unity and it's said to be equal to one third of the Qur'an because, again, the subject is Unity: 'In the name of God, the gracious, most merciful. Say he is Allah, the One, Allah, the sole Lord of all. He neither bears children nor was he ever born. And like Him, there is no one.'

I think this gives you the understanding of the oneness of God.

Did you feel that you just had to cut yourself off from the life you had led before? Could you have carried on singing for example?

It wasn't necessary for me to cut myself off and, in fact, I kept on making music and I kept on singing. I was on the road but I was now a Muslim. When I finally did embrace Islam, officially if you like, I had to begin to do certain things. One of them, the most important, is prayer. You pray five times a day and this had an incredible effect on my life because the relationship with God, the closeness that you feel, has to begin with prayer — how else do you communicate with God? So that starts to develop your God-consciousness. Then you find that you can't do the same things you used to do because you know that God has made it clear for you that this is what you should do and this what you shouldn't do. You start to make a way in your life and you start to go away from those things which are dangerous. Take, for example, singing on stage. It's obvious that music isn't forbidden in Islam, but showing off is. It contradicts your belief that there is only One to be worshipped. Any idea that would lead to some kind of human worship or idolisation is bad. Being on a stage and having spotlights on you, is slightly more innocent but you've got to be very careful, so I withdrew from public performances. I just continued to make records. But after a while, I lost my interest in music, I was more interested in studying Islam, and that's what I did.

It's a very formal code, a very strict code, in the Qur'an. Does it shackle you in a way? It lays down so clearly how you must lead your life. It does seem to cut out a lot of human free will.

Well I would say it's the opposite. People that go round saying that they're free, that they've got free will — are they free? They are free to go on making mistakes. But if you choose to follow God's way, it doesn't mean that you're giving up your free will, it means that you're submitting your will to God's will. That I think, is something to do with controlling yourself. So many people think they are free when in fact they are lost because they have no rules to guide them. It helps to know where you are going. The basic rule in Islam which I don't think many people know is that everything is allowed except those things which are forbidden. That's a completely different way of looking at it. That's the way it is in Islam. For instance, all food is permitted except for pork or dead meat, meat which has died by itself naturally. So if you look at it the other way round, we're free to do anything so long as it doesn't go against the rules.

How did your colleagues and the people you were working with in the music business react when you embraced Islam?

I was studying the Qur'an before my acceptance. I was withdrawing from the social circuit if you like, because I didn't like it. I'd never liked receptions. I always had to be rather drunk to go on with them.

I was withdrawing and my friends thought I was acting rather strangely. Here I was, carrying this book with me everywhere and going into my room and reading. Of course, you've got to realise that a lot of my friends had been with me for a long time. They knew my lyrics, my character and they knew I was searching. Perhaps they did think, 'Oh, this is just a passing phase, this is just something which he is going through.'

If it's 1971 it must be the turn of Islam?

But that of course, has been proved wrong. No one really enters Islam to leave it. There's no wish to go anywhere else.

Have any of your friends followed you into the world of Islam?

I still have very good relations with my friends from my previous career. I still have business associates, for instance, accountants and so on. I wouldn't say they have embraced

Islam as I have but they have come to understand the message of Islam which I think is very important. If you're not searching desperately for a way of life you first of all must look at things in their perspective and a lot of people have been misjudging Islam because of the way it's been presented — usually by non-Muslims.

I think a lot of people are frightened of the revelation of Islam because they see the Ayatullah and they are terrified of what he's doing in his Holy war.

You've got to remember that this is one particular event which is happening in history to a certain section of the Muslim community; I would say about four percent of Islam. You're judging all Islam by this. I don't say everything that he is doing is right, I say that you have to look at it in contrast to what there was before. The reaction of coming from an oppressive regime such as the Shah, has its effect. But then again, I wouldn't agree with everything. In Islam you have the word of God which is for all people. It's not particular to any time or space so therefore whatever anyone does in the name of Islam has to be judged by the Qur'an and by the revelation of God. The point which I think has been overlooked is that you have to stop looking at the Muslims and start looking at Islam and for that you have to go back to the original Islam. The meaning of Islam comes from Salam. Islam itself means surrender or peace with God and the example we have is the life of the Prophet, peace be upon him. People should not be frightened of something they don't know but try to find out about it. Islam is to be found in the Qur'an and the Sunnah; the Sunnah means 'the way of the Prophet'.

And yet people who will undoubtedly be able to see the peace and calmness that you've achieved through Islam, might find it hard to equate the lyrics of peace that you wrote about on your road, on

your quest, and the example of the system of Islamic justice which
seems so brutal – amputation for thieves, for example.

Well, if you go to Saudi Arabia, where there is the Islamic
law, you'll very rarely find anyone with only one hand.
What you will find, and what I've seen with my own eyes,
is people leaving when the time for prayer comes, leaving
their shops wide open — just putting a little sheet on
top — going to prayer, coming back and everything being
in its place; people leaving bags in the middle of the street.
Over here people are saying 'Oh, it's such a harsh punish-
ment', but what is the effect? What does it do? It actually
protects the innocent and it punishes the guilty, whereas
what you find in European society is that it protects the
guilty and it punishes the innocent. And that's the balance.
If we make up laws, we're bound to make mistakes but God
doesn't make mistakes. When he decrees something it's
good for the majority. That's the way we have to view it. I
think that that's very important.

Do you see yourself as having some sort of divine mission then?

Well everyone of us has a divine mission — every human
being has been created to worship and serve God. In a way I
may be fulfilling my mission a little bit more than someone
else, but in the concept as we see it in Islam, all people are
servants of God whether they are obeying or disobeying.

Couldn't you have done more though, couldn't you have spread
the message more widely if you'd adhered to your faith of Islam
but spread the message using the talents of music and lyric
writing and the performance of Cat Stevens?

Again you come to the point of how do you follow
Islam — do you follow it your way or do you follow it the
way it should be followed? Does a person come to religion
to suit himself or must he change himself to the religion?

And as I believe that Islam is not just a religion, it is actually the nature, the best nature, the best code of life for the human being, then it means that you must change your way of life to that in order to achieve what you want. So if there is music in Islam it'll come after I've learnt what Islam is. People come to Islam only for sincere reasons and not for any other reason.

Yusuf Islam, thank you very much.

P.J.KAVANAGH

P.J.KAVANAGH was born in 1931 and having studied at the Lycée Jaccard, Lausanne, he completed his education at Merton College, Oxford where he obtained his M.A. Writer and actor, he has published six collections of poems, various novels and books for children and he was awarded the Guardian Fiction Prize for *A Song and Dance*. His relationship with his first wife and her tragic death which is referred to in this interview, is recorded in the autobiographical account, *The Perfect Stranger*, which won the Richard Hillary Prize. He now lives in the Gloucestershire countryside where he pursues his particular interest in the English mystic poets and the writings of Dr. Johnson. He recently edited the *Collected Works* of Ivor Gurney and writes regularly for *The Spectator*.

Interviewed by Eric Robson

Did you have a religious basis to your life? Did you have a religious childhood?

It depends what one means by religious, but the short answer certainly is yes. I never found it difficult to believe in God. I found it difficult to believe in other people's idea of God but I always seemed to have a very firm one of my own. Whether that is a personality defect, I have no idea but I discovered at an early age that I couldn't argue with it. It was how I was made.

A lot of people experience in their lives what they choose to call love. Your relationship with Sally seems to have had an intensely spiritual dimension. Did you think of it that way at the time?

Not exactly in those terms. I found it mysterious and I find the mysterious exciting; I always have found the mysterious indicative of a truth or a reality that lies somewhere the other side of the mystery and seemed a part of it.

You described her as the 'perfect stranger'. What is the significance of that title?

Well, if you think of life as a form of journey, one is looking on the journey for experiences which somehow coincide with some idea in yourself, which comes from who knows where, of what should be. And when you meet somebody who nearly coincides with a pre-formed image, it is a stranger found in the course of the journey which one recognises. It's another form of mystery really.

It was after Sally's death that you had your moment of revelation. Can you tell me how it happened?

Well, there were several revelations and what is remarkable about them and what I'd like to stress from the outset, is how ordinary they seemed at the time. And how recognisable.

47

I suppose the first was in the hospital in Java, when I learnt that Sally was dying. I went out of the room for a moment and sat under a tree. It wasn't a visual experience but it's best described in visual terms. It was as though streams of connections of light were going from cloud to cloud. Everything seemed connected. It wasn't an aural experience either but if you can imagine choirs of angels, the music of the spheres, they were present. And what was really surprising about it was that there seemed enormous vats of consolation. Everything was all right, absolutely everything was all right. It was of immense warmth. This came as no surprise; it seemed as though one had always known that. And it was only afterwards that I realised that I hadn't thought, 'My goodness! This is a revelation, an illumination!'

I think the only point in talking about these things is so that other people can perhaps recognise moments in their own lives, of an equivalent kind and not be embarrassed or frightened by them, but trust them. The extraordinary thing was that there was nothing in that tremendous, unbelievable demonstration of warmth, of warmth in creation, that would remit the pain, no forgetting of the sort of tunnel one was going to walk down afterwards. The pain was included in the consolation. So it wasn't any form of opting out or avoidance. Nevertheless, it was like an enormous promise.

That was the first of a series of moments, intense moments, which occurred over what sort of period?

As I look back on them now, I suppose it was a series — one has to be very careful not to exaggerate or to tidy up and make a narrative out of something. After I went back to England things were very bad for me. But I think within quite a short time, after about two months, I suddenly realised I was seeing colours in a very heightened form —

things vibrated. I was seeing colours, not in a magical but perhaps in a mysterious way. You remember Blake says, 'If the doors of perception were cleansed we would see everything as it is, infinite'. And that's how I seemed to be seeing it.

Can you remember where you were when you saw this heightened colour?

Well, the first time was in Oxfordshire and could be explained psychologically, medically or pathologically. I had shortly before, come back from a year in Java where the greens are very unvarying. I was standing on a bridge by a stream and suddenly I was overwhelmed with a love for England which I'd never felt before — I'd been escaping from England as much as I could. And in this variety of greens, the extraordinary subtleness of these greens, I felt again this whole vibration of life, this beneficence, which in no way denied the fact that inside those greens, things were eating each other and that if I fell into the steam, I'd drown, and so on. Normal commonplace reality was not for a moment mitigated or taken away but nevertheless, there was this extraordinary promise.

You don't think it was simply the body's own defence mechanism saying you were in an intense moment of despair? Something inside giving you a local anaesthetic?

All those ideas came later when examining myself. I've not really talked about them very much and I've preferred to write about them obliquely because one never quite knows what one is saying. The danger is one clutches on to consolation too firmly. One is scared, one is unhappy, and so on. But it seemed these experiences went on. They didn't only happen in the countryside, they happened in London too. I remember looking at an advertisement hoarding where the paper had peeled off. I stopped in front of it and I just thought that the colours, the faded colours, were so incredibly beautiful and patient; as if it was willing to wait for ever for someone to notice it. There was something about the impersonal, non-hostility of the world and the beauty of it, the vibrating beauty of it. And then something particularly strange happened, which again, I didn't regard as strange at the time; I regarded it as absolutely commonplace. It could be described as a form of controlled hysteria.

When one has been bereaved, one is very tenderised and I saw very few people other than close friends. One of the friends took me to a party; I didn't want to go because I knew I wasn't ready for that sort of thing and I didn't know anybody there. It was a sort of late fifties, early sixties party, a kind of arty, dark, ambitious, sexy sort of party. I was standing there and everybody was talking very loudly and drinking. I realised then, I was back in the world. I'd been in the world of myself and my own loss, musing about it. Now I was back in the world, nobody was going to be nice to me; nobody was looking after me any more, I was on my own. And one would have expected a sort of Heronimus Bosch show of greed and lust. I was looking at the people, all totally involved with themselves, and I realised I didn't feel that at all. I didn't feel anything very much and then suddenly I was filled with a kind of bubbling well of laughter: I don't think I laughed out loud, I can't remember. It was a well of absolute Mozartian laughter. Inexhaustible. I was filled like a jug with this laughter. It wasn't laughter *at* the people, it wasn't laughter *at* myself. There was no self in it for a moment. It was just laughter. And then it subsided and I felt cleansed throughout, sort of drenched, as one can occasionally feel after a burst of weeping — as I say, it might be an hysterical thing, but it was beautiful, undeniably beautiful.

Again, exactly the same as the time before, there was no surprise in it. I wasn't watching, I wasn't aware of myself, I wasn't saying, 'this is extraordinary — this is happening to me'. It was only afterwards one realised that it had never happened to one before; now I'm in a position to say, 'it's never happened to me since'.

You say at the time you felt that it was very commonplace and down to earth. Have you ever thought that some divine presence was in contact with you, at those moments?

So much of the core of the experience seems to me not to have to do with myself: that the trouble is myself. And what the experiences had in common was the sudden release from self. Then I thought, well obviously, hyperaesthesia, hysteria, mechanisms of self protection released by nature. I thought of this and all those things I can accept as being true, perhaps the final explanation. But in answer to your question, what has seemed absolutely clear to me is that if one is presented with something which is undeniably beautiful and true, then one has a choice. One can either trust that, or trust one's experience of one's ordinary self; one's ordinary reality. And I have no difficulty in trusting the insight as being the truth.

What do you think was being imparted to you? Or what signpost to your life, do you think you were being given?

Well, it sounds an absolutely insane thing to say, in what Dr. Johnson called 'this world bursting with sin and sorrow' — which indeed it is — but I would say, consolation. A reality that for reasons that I know not of, we are kept from but, occasionally, are allowed to glimpse and by which we should be guided.

Perhaps because of the heightened emotional state you were in, you actually let the barrier drop?

Yes, exactly. I think every man and woman has their own moment. I think this is a much more commonplace series of experiences although it would tend to be different for each personality. One of the troubles of our present secular century, especially in England where the great disease is embarrassment, is that you can't mention these things to anybody.

Also, there is a curious fashion that the only reality is the unpleasant. In fact the more unpleasant something is, the more real it is. And we tend to cut ourselves off from these moments of consolation. Even the word consolation, is regarded as rather wet. But consolation is there, that I do believe.

You're a poet, you're an author, you obviously get inspiration at moments which lead you through your writing. Were those moments of revelation in any way like the moments of literary inspiration?

Oh yes, exactly the same. Of greater intensity but exactly the same. Things coming together; things making sense. Sometimes words come into a certain pattern which is right. You know it's right. And it was as simple as that. Yes, the two things are very connected.

Do you believe that all of us can experience it? I sit in this chair week after week, talking with people yet never having had one of these moments of revelation.

I bet you have — you just weren't looking. How could it not be so? To think otherwise would make one say one was a special person. What is absolutely apparent within these illuminations — I prefer to call them that rather than revelations because they seem to contain light and warmth — is that one feels human rather than personal. A part of creation.

Do you think it's possible to harness these illuminations? A sort of psychic windmill or psychic turbine.

I dare say it might be possible for some. Blake said, 'One has to create a system or be enslaved by another'. I rather dislike systems. I think they can have their role but to harness them is using the wrong part of one's mind — one's reason. As you say, like harnessing water for power and so on. I think life is tougher than that; I think you have to soldier on and use what rations you're very occasionally given. Why it should be so, I don't know but I believe with Keats, that 'the world is a vale of soul making' and sometimes one is given this little bun.

Have you never been tempted to go on a quest for further illumination, further moments of revelation?

I do it all the time, doesn't everybody? I mean when one is moving about looking at things and speaking to people, one's in attendance, isn't one?

Has it led you to God in a new way?

Oh, yes. All these phrases are terrible but yes, it has. The key seems to me to be Christianity. It seems to include all these experiences. As I said, I don't really like systems but it has slowly become clear to me that some kind of formal concentration or social concentration, some form of prosaic habit is necessary. Therefore, reluctantly but finally, I've come round to the idea of formal church — and of going to it.

It isn't immediately obvious to me why you draw the connection between what you experienced and Christianity.

Because Christianity contains all these things. It contains this promise. It contains forgiveness, it contains the idea that 'one has to get some service in'. One has to work at it. It isn't easy for anybody but we're all in it together. It contains all sorts of things like that and also of course it has the liturgy. I know they've been mucking about with the liturgy but so long as the vicar or the priest doesn't talk too much, so long as he keeps out of it, this heightened language which is sometimes very unspecific, marvellously unspecific, lets this tradition speak. I'm a great believer in tradition, in accumulated wisdom. All one's experiences can be canalized into this and enlarged because there's never any meanness, there's never any restriction.

I'm not talking about the behaviour of churches when they're in charge of a State. I'm certainly not talking about the behaviour of the Catholic church in the 16/17th century. But the Christian tradition contains, enlarges, makes you more generous in your connection with other people. Private revelations tend to move inwards and get hugged and also get very muddied. One needs the tradition to keep oneself clear and practical and unneurotic.

You see, I could imagine someone who's had that series of experiences, being tempted perhaps to go in the direction of an Eastern religion which includes these things – but that isn't so in terms of Christianity, is it?

Oh, I would have thought it was. Everybody has to find their own path, I suppose, but I think an awful lot of us live far too much in reaction: we live far too much in reaction against our parents and far too much in reaction against history. We want to make ourselves special, we want to make ourselves something. If you have parents who go to church, you become a Buddhist or something — why not, so long as you are clear in your mind? I mean one has to be clear one isn't doing it for any extraneous reason like shocking one's parents or being different from other people. I would have thought the revelation given to western Europe and western European culture mixed with the Judaic is my bag, my culture. There's no reason for me to go seeking strange gods.

P. J. Kavanagh, thank you very much.

KRISHNAMURTI

JIDDU KRISHNAMURTI was born in India in 1895 amidst astrological predictions of a saintly destiny. He was discovered by the Theosophists, Annie Besant and C.W. Leadbeater, who observed that 'his Aura had not a particle of selfishness in it'. Brought to England in 1911, he was intensively groomed and paraded as the imminent 'World Teacher', a role he totally rejected in 1929. Although he avoids reference to his past spiritual experiences, he has continued to teach and write, and he is followed by thousands of people throughout the world who seek for spiritual freedom.

Interviewed by Eric Robson

Throughout your life people have regarded you as special. Can you remember what it was like as a child of fourteen to be plucked from obscurity?

I'm afraid I don't remember. Actually I was rather shy. I avoided it all. I didn't like all the personal worship; being looked up to as a great man and all that kind of thing. As I grew up I avoided crowds. When I was asked to speak in a public meeting, I was so shy, I tried to speak behind a curtain and that didn't work out so I came out from behind the curtain and talked. Probably I've really led a rather lonely life. Not lonely in the sense of being apart, but keeping away from all the noise, all the fuss and all the absurdities.

Did you ever believe, as the people who were sponsoring you believed, that you were some sort of messiah?

I never bothered about it really. It sounds rather funny but seriously, I never bothered about it. Who I was, what I was — it's not really important. I was given a great many properties all over the world including a castle in Holland with five thousand acres. I returned all that. I didn't believe, and still don't believe, in organised religious structures or a hierarchical attitude towards life.

But before you gave back the properties, before you renounced the position that your sponsors were putting you in, you had experienced in California what to many people, might be described as a revelation. You saw a roadman* and you felt that

---

* In 1922 Krishnamurti had two experiences which changed his life. Of the first he wrote, 'There was a man mending the road; that man was myself; the pick axe he held was myself . . . I could feel the wind passing through the tree, and the little ant on the blade of grass, I could feel . . . I was in everything or rather everything was in me, inanimate and animate, the mountain, the worm and all breathing things.'

The following day he experienced 'such a profound calmness both in

57

*you were part of him, part of the hammer that he had in his hand
and part of the road.*

I don't know how to put it clearly to you. There is a great
tradition among the seriously religious people, that you
must go through various forms of self-purification: not by
starving, fasting and all that torturing of the body but a
sense of inward cleansing, as it were; a purification of mind
that is not self-centred, that is not concerned with personal
progress, personal achievement and all such ambitions. I
think it was and it still is, a part of a deep religious feeling. It
is not the abandonment of the whole world but a small part
of it.

*Was that what you realised when you saw the road mender and
when you stood under the pepper tree and experienced what I
think you described as a supreme happiness?*

Yes, more than happiness — happiness is really a side
issue — much more a sense of wholeness.

*Was it that sense of wholeness which came from those experiences
that eventually led you to break with your sponsors and, as you
told us, reject the adulation, reject the position they were trying to
put you in?*

They weren't trying to put me in there. They really
believed it all. Doctor Besant, the first woman who talked
about divorce and birth control, absolutely believed what
she said. It was not a facade; it was a real deep faith in her.

---

the air and within myself, the calmness of the bottom of a deep unfathomable lake. Like the lake I felt my physical body with its mind and motions
could be ruffled on the surface but nothing, nay nothing, could disturb
the calmness of my soul ... Nothing could ever be the same. I have drunk
of the clear and pure waters at the source of the fountain of life and my
thirst was appeased.'
    From *Krisnamurti: The Years of Awakening* by Mary Lutyens, John
Murray Ltd.

Was there any moment when you realised you had to break from it?

No, I don't think so. It was a natural process. It wasn't just one moment and then everything was clear.

You have already mentioned your positive objection to organised religions, can you explain to us why you are so positively against these things?

How can you organise a human being according to a pattern? How can you shape a man who is extraordinarily alive, to a particular mould of a religious pattern, faith, belief, dogma or rituals? This is what the communists are trying to do. The communists, the totalitarians, are trying to force man into a certain way of thinking, which is so contrary to freedom. Man has always sought throughout history, to be free. This is one of his urgent and constant demands, to be free: not only from poverty, environmental ugliness and so on but to be free from sorrow, pain and anxiety. And how can any structured religious attitude give him freedom? I know there are seven hundred million Catholics in the world. Their whole structure is based on faith, but among the ancient Hindus and Buddhists it was a tenet that you must doubt, you must question, you must enquire, never accept authority, especially in spiritual matters. I, therefore, apply this to other structures.

Is that also the reason why you reject faith as a concept?

Yes. Why do we need faith and all the rituals? Why project some figure, some idea and then have to have faith in it? It all seems rather unnecessary.

The Ten Commandments, they're presumably not a bad set of rules by which to live your life? If you abide by them you'll live quite a good life. Would you accept that?

Yes, but the whole fact of obedience to some edict, whether

a religious sanction or legalistic action, imparts a sense of fear. If man is allowed to do what he likes, whatever he likes he does. So why have all the structures imposed on human minds? Why not tackle freedom directly? In the totalitarian states and the so called democratic states, human beings are doing exactly what they like in spite of faith.

Because people who adhere to organised religion would probably say that the human being is weak, he needs guidance, he needs discipline, without which all is darkness, all is anarchy.

But have we discipline now? Do we not have terrible chaos, violence and brutality, and appalling suffering, in the world? In this country there are three and a half million unemployed. In India and other parts of the world, there is tremendous poverty, in spite of affluent societies and in spite of industrial advance. I think we are talking about a much deeper issue than merely imposing something on the human brain and saying, 'look, stick to that'.

So what is your alternative?

Human beings have always been self-centred, always selfish. Various religions have tried to help man not to be so self-centred; to identify himself with something greater. But the greater is still part of selfishness. And so I think one should really begin with self-knowledge. The ancient Hindus, long before the Greeks, said 'Know Thyself'. If you don't understand yourself fundamentally, whatever you do will still be the activity of illusions. So, 'Know Thyself'. Not according to some philosopher or psychologist but know yourself in your relationship with the world and the intimate relationship with those with whom you live. Relationship is like a mirror, in which you see yourself directly as you are. No pretentions, watch your reactions, understand your reactions and go beyond. It's a complex human structure, the human mind. So begin with yourself. Not that it emphasises self-centredness but in knowing yourself, you are going beyond yourself. To really enquire requires a great deal of responsibility. Understand that you are not isolated but are a part of the world — that you are not a separate human being. You are like the rest of humanity: you suffer, humanity suffers. You are anxious, everyone in the world is anxious. Fear, depression, is shared by all human beings, whatever their colour. So begin with yourself. And then you'll find your relationship with the world is not only holistic but it transcends and goes beyond the personal limited activity of the self.

Is your system rooted in any religion?

Of course not. System is again a pattern; obedience to a pattern, obedience to a certain ideal, has led to such enormous conflict. Look what's happening now. The ideals of the communists and of the democratic worlds, are in conflict. So really one has to ask, what place have ideals in life? They may have no place at all. What is important is to begin with what is actual.

I think you wrote in one of your books, that an idealist is a hypocrite.

Yes. Idealists are really dangerous people because they identify themselves with an ideal. For instance, they identify themselves with non-violence which is an ideal, not a fact and yet they become violent. We have all seen this.

That isn't always the case, is it? I could think of examples of social reformers who identified themselves with an ideal or a campaign which didn't lead to bloodshed or conflict.

In some cases it may not but in other cases it may. So the real question is: why do human beings, throughout the world, live in conflict? Not only with themselves but with almost everything — with nature, with their wives, with their husbands, with their neighbours? Why? That's really the fundamental question.

Surely you have a system or a method to transfer what you believe to people?

We are talking freely now — enquiring, investigating — there is no system. We are both concerned about something and we discuss it: we do not need a system. We are concerned about the conflict which is destroying the world. Is it possible to live without conflict? Is it possible to live a life of great love and to be free from suffering? By enquiring, we discover a great many things. If we both listen and watch carefully, we will discover the most fantastic and real things and the perception of that brings us together. There is no you or me, just perception.

You have written that before one can achieve this state, before one can achieve this perception, we have to strip away the conditioning that we all suffer. Have you stripped away your Hindu conditioning?

Long ago. It meant nothing to me really — whether to be a Hindu, a Moslem or a Christian. Those are all human brains which have been programmed like computers.

How do you strip away the conditioning?

To answer that, we must first discover the answer to this question: Is there a difference between you and your conditioning? You say, how can I strip away my conditioning? If there is a you and a conditioning there is a division. But the you is conditioned. The problem is not you and conditioning. There is only conditioning. We have grown into the habit of thinking of me and the conditioning as though I must do something about it — as though I were different from it. When there is that division, there is conflict and that conflict is totally unnecessary and false. The you and the conditioning are the same. The observer is the observed.

Say, for example, human beings are frightened of fear — fear of death, of living, of tomorrow, of insecurity. From primitive man to the present time, man has had fear and has always tried to overcome and run away from it. But the I is fear and fear can be watched. Now, is there an observation of this fear without division? The I, the self, who is the watcher, includes the past; past memories, past incidents, past recognitions, and that past looks upon the present as though it were something separate from itself. And then there is conflict.

Would I be simplistic and naive if I said the end result is total unity?

I don't know what you mean by total unity.

Yourself, fear, everything becomes one.

Could we use the word consciousness? Consciousness is all the biological reactions, physical reactions, emotional reactions and intellectual concepts — all the intellectual philosophy — fear, faith, God or no God, dogma, scepticism, anxiety, depression, pleasure, sorrow — it is all part of consciousness. That consciousness is me or you. Now that being so, then every human being, at whatever state of evolution or education, goes through this. He suffers anxiety, insecurity, searching for security, quarrelling — conflict, pain, sorrow, this is common to all human beings. So we are human beings, not an 'I' separated from a 'You'.

Is there only one truth or are there many truths? Is what you've been telling me, the only truth?

There is only one Truth: not Moslem truth, Christian truth or Hindu or Buddhist. There is only Truth.

But people find their way to what they believe is the truth, in many different ways. For example, the Christian saints arrived at what they saw as the truth through Christ. May I read to you something which was written by Mozart? 'My soul opened out as it were into the infinite; the deep that my own struggle had opened up within my being, answered by the unfathomable deep without, reaching beyond the stars. I stood along with him who made me and felt the perfect union of my spirit with his. It was like the effect of some orchestra when all the separate notes have melted into one swelling harmony. The darkness held a presence. I could not any more have doubted that He was there, than I was.'

First of all, would you agree that truth has no path? It's not a Christian path, a Hindu path or a Communist path, so it's a pathless land. If truth were fixed then there would be a path to it. But it's a living thing and each one interprets it according to his own conditioning. They generally agree truth is universal — obviously any thinking man does. But suppose one has been brought up as a Christian, you translate that truth according to what you have been programmed to think. Mozart in his way was conditioned. And the Hindu, the Moslem and the Sikh. So the question really is whether one can be totally free of this conditioning and have a mind that's completely free from all programming.

But doesn't that lead us to a paradox; in this pathless land of truth, people who come to your school, the people who listen to you speak in California or India or Switzerland, regard you as a signpost in a pathless land?

I have always said there is no authority including myself: I'm not your leader, Guru and all that nonsense. I really mean it. For that's an abomination to me, that's original sin. Each man must be a light to himself because freedom is necessary. Freedom from all the trivia of that part of our consciousness. Who is going to lead you to that freedom? The Buddhists will say Lord Buddha, the Hindus something else and the Christians will say Jesus Christ, and so on. And they are all in conflict with each other. It's so obviously false. I reject all that because to me, in matters of the mind and matters of the spirit, there is no leader. There is no person who says 'do this' and 'don't do that'.

But can someone who speaks as powerfully as you speak, who thinks as deeply as you think, avoid being a leader to lesser men?

At every talk, at every discussion I say this: 'Don't do it, be careful, don't follow'. Its so silly because you are destroying yourself by following. What Krishnamurti is talking about may be utterly false. Begin with scepticism, don't accept anything, including what I'm saying. Work it out, let's discuss it, let's go into it together. So that there is no you as the leader and I the follower. We are together in this business of living.

Can I ask you what happens when you approach the pathless land of truth, when you step over the boundaries and find yourself there, do you have to do anything with that truth or does it just do it for you?

There is a story of two men who have been friends for a long time. One day as they are walking along the road, one of them picks up something, looks at it, and his whole face is absolutely changed — radiant. The other says, 'What the dickens has happened to you?' He replies, 'I have picked up something which is part of truth; it's most marvellous.' And the other fellow says, 'Wonderful! Now let's go and organise it.' Or look at it another way. What is love? Obviously love is not jealousy, love is not hate, love is not pleasure nor desire. No, if you negate all that which is not love, then love will act. You don't have to say, 'what will it do?' If you are intelligent and have a sense of deep communication with all human beings, your action will be entirely different. Where it goes wrong is when we begin to say, 'show me first', and then do something else! 'I want the guarantee first.'

But people do want guarantees, don't they?

I know, that's just it.

Can anyone achieve this truth?

If they apply their mind and their heart to it.

Can you understand that people can be frightened of this? Whatever religion they may have, you want to destroy the icons and trust the truth that's there. How do you explain to people who have that fear?

The ultimate fear is death — and the whole world is frightened of death. Death means burning icons. Why don't we live every day with death, burning the icons that we build? If I'm told that I'm going to die this evening I may be frightened for the moment but I arrange everything; I think, I'll put this away or keep that, throw all this out, for I know I'm going to meet death at the end of the day. When there is a crisis I'm not frightened. It's only thinking about the crises which is frightening. Thinking about death is frightening.

I think fear is merely a continuity of time and thought. Thinking that I'm going to die this evening, in five, ten years' time or the next day: thinking causes fear. And thinking that time is tomorrow. Both time and thought are the factors of fear. The present contains all time. So in the present, in the 'Now', all time is contained. When there is this understanding of time and death, then I'm living with death all the time — not frightened of it.

You've said you believe that the world can only change through this personal transformation; and yet, the world seems to be sliding to the edge of the black abyss. Won't this personal transformation come too late?

Transformation means moving from one form to another form. I don't mean transformation but radical psychological revolution. You change radically in that sense and you're going to affect the world. It might be very little, but you are going to affect it. Take a bad case like Hitler. He was insane yet affected the whole world. So I think if a few of us radically changed, there could be a tremendous effect, quite naturally.

We've used the phrase 'the truth' a lot in this conversation of ours: is there a simple way of describing what the truth is?

You cannot measure the immeasurable by words. So don't measure truth. I'm not dodging it, but you can't describe it, you can't put it into words anymore than I can put the universe into a telescope. So I think first one must stop. It is necessary to understand the whole question of measurement because we're always measuring. To transcend measurement we need to meditate. Meditation is being free of measurement. That's the essence of meditation, the essence of having no comparison.

Krishnamurti, thank you very much.

SARAH MILES

SARAH MILES was born in Essex in 1942 and was educated at Roedean and Crofton Grange. She trained as an actress at RADA and began her career with the Worthing Repertory Company. She played the lead opposite Laurence Olivier in *Term of Trial*, joined The National Theatre and went on to star in such films as: *Those Magnificent Men in their Flying Machines*, *The Servant*, *The Hireling* and *Ryan's Daughter*. She now lives just outside London where she is working on a book which describes in greater detail the experience given in this interview.

Interviewed by Eric Robson

Do you have memories of your early childhood?

Yes. I spend a lot of time in silence. I regressed through to my childhood in silence, to try to gain a slight amount of self-knowledge. I think you can only do it by going back, if you can, to your memories of the past. Some people claim to go right back to the womb: I can't claim that. My first memories were of bars of a cot, cat net and lattice windows and I knew I wanted to get back to where I'd come from because, wherever I'd been, was really quite beautiful. And then, I suppose I learned to walk and that memory, or that need to return to where I'd come from, disappeared. My childhood was blissfully content; we lived deep in the countryside, there was no television in those days and I think it was idyllic in every sense of the word. We weren't poor, so in fact everything was as it should be for childhood. I was wrapped up and protected by a fearlessness; a harmony with nature and farmyard animals.

But as a child, did you experience fear?

I did have a problem of not eating when I was a little girl: I didn't like food terribly much and, of course, my parents were worried about that. My father used to read me bedtime stories and there was one from the fables of Struvvel Petre, about 'Augustus' who wouldn't eat his soup. The drawings showed him getting thinner and thinner until he ended up in the ground with a cross on the top of him and his soup bowl next to the cross. I asked Daddy, 'What's happened to Augustus?' and he said, 'Well, he's under the ground, he's gone.' I said, 'You can't breathe under the ground.' He said, 'No, you don't breathe when you are dead.' I remember distinctly that moment when it became known to me that I would die. It gave me a raw fear — I think an unnatural fear — and all my energy went into fear of death, certainly for quite a long time. There wasn't any way of overcoming it. I thought it was the normal state of things and it remained with

71

me until I went to boarding school. We were in dormitories then and because I was with other girls I didn't feel that fear, so raw and terrifying. It gradually left me as sexual awareness came into my life. Then the fear of death completely disappeared.

So did you turn to sexuality to overcome these earlier doubts?

Well, I certainly wasn't plotting to do this. I just noticed in retrospect, that my fear of death was blotted out by the awareness of sexual feelings.

Did that overcome self doubt and lack of confidence as well?

No, I don't think so. The Press have made me out to be some sort of sex maniac; they identify me with the roles that I've played on the screen. Obviously I was young and I liked it. But I think we're born, we're here to create or reproduce and we die. Because I was in the area of coming into reproduction, which is what making love is about, perhaps that is why the fear of death subsided.

And yet, the Sarah Miles's sexuality is not ordinary sexuality it seems. So many people have perceived it as something different.

Well, that's their fault!

Would you agree with the analysis that some people believe that Sarah Miles has an almost mystical sexual attraction?

I can't answer that, it's so dangerous. I don't quite know what you mean by it and I'm sure I don't have it.

But people have been so drawn to you. Men throughout your early career were drawn by this mystical sexual power of yours.

I suppose that might be true. But it never gave me any pleasure. I noticed it in a way but it was never particularly comforting because it's something that I'm not aware of myself. I didn't know what it was in me that produced this effect on others and I think that's probably a lot to do with the mistakes I made.

But when you saw the effect it was having on others, did you ever come to believe it was a malevolent power?

This is a lot to do with what happened later, when I retreated altogether. I had to find out what it was that had caused the chaos in my wake.

Did you have any religious belief that was able to help you through that devastating and traumatic part of your life?

No. I have no religion. I never have had a religion. I think religion segregates and divides us all where spirituality binds and nurtures us all. But at that time, I was closed off; I became numb and ice. I cut off the pain. I didn't deal with events as I should. I cut off and that's what causes cancer; I was very lucky not to get it. All that time I was ignorant of spirituality.

You went on to make the film, The Sailor Who Fell From Grace with the Sea, *a very sexually explicit film. Why did you agree to do another film like this?*

I did it because I'm an actress and need to work. There wasn't much money involved with that film because it was an art film. It was the philosophy of Misheema. It is a very powerful philosophy. He believed that you should die at your peak, that you mustn't continue using air and water and food that belongs to others when you have nothing left in you. That's what the film's about. You die at your full potential, like a ripe apple that you sever and open to the light. It has a moment of glory rather than dying within the core and withering. To cut yourself off at your peak is a tough philosophy to understand.

Did you find the scenes in that film, an echo of what had been said about you, or did you feel that you were on a much higher level than that?

Yes. I did see it on a higher level because of Misheema himself. He was an extraordinary man and I think the script did a brilliant job of bringing the East to the West. The film also dealt with masturbation which is a subject I felt quite strongly about at that time. As a child, I was told that masturbation was evil, that my hair would fall out and I'd go blind. I thought it would be a good opportunity to do it for everybody to see and to try and make it elegant and beautiful. In fact, it really isn't an ugly act because you are giving yourself a release and you're not causing harm to a living soul by doing it. So I thought I could do my little humble bit of putting some people's doubts at rest. But I wasn't quite aware of the ugly pit I'd dug for myself; it is such a lonely act. A male director can't tell a woman how to masturbate; something that we all do in private. So I had no help with it and the crew were people I'd known from way back on other films, they'd never had to shoot a mastur-bation scene before, so we were all feeling awkward and I realised, it was totally up to me. It was a very lonely pit I'd dug for myself. I wanted to make it beautiful and not ugly, yet true, so I was lonely doing it. In fact, I think it was the only lonely moment in my life.

It was shortly after that, wasn't it, that you had the first revelation?

Yes, it was. I'd done the scene and I went home feeling distressed because of the pain of the loneliness of doing it. The next night when I saw the rushes, I knew that I'd done a fairly good job. It was one of the few moments in which I felt I'd most succeeded. As soon as the rushes came to an end, they all came around to say, 'Well done'. I said, 'Goodnight, see you tomorrow' and went out of the rushes theatre and I began to walk home. I was living in a little cottage on the edge of the Dart estuary. It was evening, I was walking along the road and there was nobody about.

Can you explain to me what happened?

It was quite beautiful. I had enormous heat coming from an area just above the solarplexus. It was a fierce heat from the centre, like fire, hot fire, hotter even than fire. I also noticed that I was numb in my extremities, my feet were cold and I was icy but boiling in the centre. My breath seemed to be coming from a place that I'd never known it come from before. I felt fear because of this heat and then it changed. I was doubtless. There was no doubt, there was an aching of strength that passeth all understanding. I felt at that moment, not I, but something else that was me, yet wasn't me, was capable of just dancing across the estuary. I felt that I could, through something else that was happening to me, do anything. It was a moment of utter doubtlessness and I think almost omnipotence. It was as if God was within and without and I was at one within and without with all things. It sounds terribly cliché'd, but it's so difficult to describe. Extraordinary doubtlessness. This was what was so strange — doubtlessness about everything and knowledge about everything.

You used an almost Biblical phrase, in your description a moment ago, 'passeth all understanding'. Did you feel at the time, that God was talking to you?

There was certainly something talking, there always has been ever since and what that something is, I'm going to find out!

Did you hear a voice?

I do hear an inner voice, at all times since then, and I follow it. I tell you something else that happened at that moment. I realised very clearly that we are eternal and I thought at the time, that from this moment on, I'm going to discover my spriritual body and eternity, rather than dwell on my physical body and death. And I have listened to the inner voice from that moment.

How long did the impact of this first of your revelations actually last?

Well, I wasn't timing it and these things are timeless because they're not dealing with time as we know it. Looking back, it could have been a minute, it could have been five minutes: the actual moment of revelation I suppose might have been a split second, the actual journey was about five minutes.

But, at the end of that journey, the effect wore off?

No it didn't. The feeling of total doubtlessness, of God-liness, remained. The heat still remained and the breathing, this strange breathing that had taken place, remained. The feeling of dancing across the water had disappeared, so I suppose the power had declined but I was still in a strange place.

During those following days, when you were obviously trying to come to terms with what had happened to you, did the doubt-lessness remain or did you gradually drift back into the pit?

Oddly enough, like the Yin and Yan, the negative and positive, the good and evil, very shortly after this magnificent moment, I went from being all powerful to being a total puppet. Something else took over when I got into my house, some other force turned me into a puppet and was telling me to do things which frightened me. The result of what happened was that I thought I was evil, that I was perhaps mad or a witch. Unfortunately, the blackness followed the light in that particular instant which was very sad. Or perhaps not; perhaps the other experience was in fact a blessing because it changed my life in a way the earlier experience might not have done.

Let's pursue the chronology of what actually happened. You had your high moment of spiritual experience, you were then thrown back into the pit and believed you could have been a witch. How did that end?

It ended horribly. I didn't want to tell the film crew or production team about any of it. It was very important that I kept it to myself and I had to finish the film. I felt I was like a walking Zombie but I don't think anybody else noticed. I just knew I wanted to get the film over, get away and be in silence to think about what had been happening to me. So the film finished and I went to look after a house for a friend of mine in Los Angeles; a very kindly woman who allowed me to live in her home when she went on tour. She thought I looked a bit odd and I said I had 'flu. She put me to bed and tucked me up and I remember waving her goodbye. I was in bed and I was frozen with the experience. Absolutely frozen by both experiences because nothing like that had ever happened to me. Quite honestly, I was very happy leading my life the way it had been going, believing that death was the end, making the best of it and doing everything I could to get the most out of life before I died. Of course, I now know that is ludicrous, but that's how I was patterning my life until that moment.

There I was, suddenly realising that the power of thought is monumental and that in me was goodness and evil. It was up to me to decide what I was going to do with this power and it upset me terribly. I didn't go for help. Something stopped me from doing this. I hung in there because something told me to. After about two days in bed I was so cold I ran a bath and lay in it for almost three days, constantly topping it up with hot water. It seemed the only place where I could keep warm. I was still very cold and I decided it was

ridiculous. A lot of thoughts came to me in the bath, like
'I've got to get on with life.' Actually, I was being drawn
towards death and now it held no fear for me. I went down
to my friend's bathroom where she kept a lot of sleeping
pills. I was absolutely certain that I was being asked to go.
Something was telling me to leave. It couldn't be worse than
what was happening here, so why not? Try whatever new
adventure there was. I put the pills into my hand and I filled
the glass, then this extraordinary thing happened — really
quite extraordinary. There was no doubt in my mind that I
would go through with it as I lifted up my hand to swallow.
As I did, I saw myself in the mirror and I saw my eyes. I saw
this heat of life, I looked at my face and it seemed to me to be
not evil, but kindly! It didn't look as evil as I felt it had
during the last few weeks. I thought, wait a minute, am I
doing the right thing? There's kindliness here and not the
evil that I was afraid was in me. Anyway, I realised I might
be making a mistake. I put the pills aside and took up paper
and pen and just wrote away, wrote away for three years.

You really broke with the world you'd known – I mean, you threw
yourself into a position of solitude, left Malibu and retreated into
the hills. What did you experience there? You had gone through
these three moments of intense experience. You then put yourself
in probably the most difficult position of being alone, and coping
with the memory of these experiences. What was it like away
from it all, just being with yourself?

Those years were necessary. I can't say they were glorious
but they were necessary for me to be able to come out at the
other end. I had to go through a lot of searching so that I
could live my life in a stronger way. I'm not saying that I'm
perfect in any way. I'm just on the very first step of the new
life. It led me to meditation and, indeed, to yoga; both of
which have served me beautifully over the years. I think
meditation is a wonderful route for people to take to gain

self-knowledge but I wish it was more enjoyable and not merely a question of self-discipline at the beginning. It is delightful later but does require a lot of self-discipline and I wish people didn't have to go through the agony that I went through.

Did your moments of revelation turn you away from the career you had? Did they persuade you that you didn't really want to be an actress any more?

It was much more important. Now that I was listening to something else that was taking me forward, I was putting myself in the hands of fate which I had never done before. I had been forcing a pattern to my life, always forcing myself to new materialistic goals and to achieving fame. My whole life had been that of the normal sort of actress trying to get ahead, so this was something completely new. You see, I was in catharsis. You must understand these had been such great shocks to my system. I had to re-assess everything. I believe that first moment as a child, when I knew I was going to die, I sub-consciously or consciously patterned my life knowing there was a deadline. You pattern it differently than you would if there was no deadline. Suddenly, I had no deadline. I knew that death was not the end. Therefore, I had a whole new patterning to do, a whole new self to create. It wasn't a question of belief — I knew it. It is knowledge. But trying to put this knowledge into practice each day is damned hard work.

Sarah Miles, thank you very much.

POSTSCRIPT

I am overwhelmed at the enormous amount of kindly correspondence I have received in response to my revelation programme.

It is so thrilling to know that the whole series seems to have served its purpose, the awakening of the seeds of spirituality which — alas — seemed to have lain dormant in most of us. The power of spirit is all.

I cannot attempt to answer all the hundreds of questions individually, but I do have a book coming out next year (1986) which will, hopefully, attempt to clarify that which was only touched upon in this interview.

IRIS MURDOCH

IRIS MURDOCH, novelist and philosopher, was born in Dublin in 1919 and completed her education in London, Bristol and Somerville College, Oxford. A Fellow of St. Anne's College and Hon. Fellow of Somerville College, Oxford, she has combined a distinguished academic career with a formidable output of brilliant novels and plays including: *A Severed Head*, *The Sea, The Sea* (Booker Prize), *The Black Prince* (James Tait Memorial Prize), *The Sacred and Profane Love Machine* (Whitbread Prize) and *The Bell*. Central to her work is a philosophical appreciation of the conflict between good and evil. Miss Murdoch, who is married to Professor John Bayley, was awarded the C.B.E. in 1976.

Interviewed by Eric Robson

Reading your books, spirituality and religion are themes that you seem to explore time and again. Does your interest in spirituality and religion come from a childhood interest?

I was brought up inside a religion. I prayed as soon as I could speak and I felt the presence of God as a child and I knew all about Christ. Indeed I knew all about the Holy Trinity when I was about six or seven years old: I mean it was extremely familiar to me. In this sense I am very deeply based inside Christianity in the Anglican Church. But I was without any intensity or anxiety: I never worried about it or felt that I was enclosed by a powerful organisation or anything of that kind. I was confirmed as an Anglican at fifteen and had a religious experience of the kind that I imagine many people have at that age.

Then it all vanished. I became a Marxist and I regarded these things as superstitions. When I ceased to be a Marxist, I felt a greater connection with religion without coming back to any particular dogma.

You've been quoted as saying that you believe in religion but not in God. What do you mean by that?

Well, it dawned on me that religion isn't a matter of holding supernatural beliefs. This word supernatural is ambiguous perhaps. I mean beliefs about heaven or survival after death or a personal God or the resurrection. I don't believe in any of these things and I think people now find it very hard to do so. But that doesn't mean that the whole of the Christian revelation is lost to me. Religion is something which is very much wider and deeper than the dogmas. Eastern religions have always said and understood this.

You've said that you consider yourself to be a Christian Buddhist.

I did go through a time when I thought of actually becoming a Buddhist and I was taught a form of meditation by Buddhists. I think it is a marvellous religion in the sense that it combines an historical root with a mystical development which doesn't demand any particular historical belief. I think the symbols or pictures of religion are very important. Obviously people can live without them — I don't mean that they're essential, but if you have a connection with religion the symbolism is moving and deep, it's a spiritual source. I find the sophisticated teaching of Buddhism attractive. You are to be saved here and now in this life and in this time: there isn't any other place for salvation.

The question can arise nowadays of how you define religion. People might say religion is really just morality dressed up, but I think an essential thing about religion — and this is something in common between Buddhism and Christianity — is the notion that you should in some sense seek salvation, that it is the task of people in this world to become good, to love unselfishly, to overcome egoism. The symbolism of Christianity — the figure of Christ whom I regard as a mystical figure like the figure of Buddha — teaches this. Christ is a real man, who was a great teacher and a great saint, but also a mystical figure who has become familiar to millions and millions of people. That is the essential thing about one's relation to these symbols: that they express the absolute importance of salvation or new being.

But if you adhere to the trappings and the symbols, and don't believe in the resurrection, if you don't believe in the spiritual dimension behind them, do they not become rather hollow?

Symbols can always be a barrier. Judaism and Christianity tell us not to bow down to graven images, and Islam takes that command very literally. These things can come in between you and your objective and be false consolations, stopping places, beyond which you don't go. You observe certain rules and you don't think of anything further. But the spiritual dimension is beyond the rules. It is able to use the images and icons and to see that they point beyond themselves. It is like a form of Platonism. Plato said that spiritual progress was the progressive breaking of images, that what you took to be reality is a shadow of something better and more real which lies further on.

But do the images, in your view, point to an external force of good or evil?

One couldn't live on this planet for long without noticing that there's a difference between good and evil and that it's terribly important! There are forces of good and evil in a perfectly ordinary sense — there are people who bring about destruction, and there is egoism from which we all suffer. Yet, sometimes one meets somebody who seems to be without egoism. One also sees it in terms of societies. One might say, all societies are bad but some societies are very much worse than others. The conflict between good and evil is the great conflict of the planet and of our lives.

I believe in good as something which arises in the soul. It's something which each person is able to recognise. I think people sometimes profess to be 'beyond good and evil' or to be so cynical that they don't see any difference; but this is just play acting. They are wanting to dissociate themselves from a particular version of the distinction. But the difference I think lives with us all. In this sense I believe the reality of good is connected with the reality of all our strivings — it's something we come across every day in all the things that we do, how we employ our time and how we think about people, whether we are able to learn difficult things and really care about other people, or whether we're selfish and satisfied with what is superficial. All the struggles that happen in the process of being a human being are connected with the reality of the struggle between good and evil, and the connection of good with the genuine, with what's true. But I would stress that I don't believe in any external presence, I don't believe in a personal God or a paradise elsewhere or anything outside humanity. It's all here in our human existence.

Yet your books repeatedly have characters using the word 'revelation'.

I think that in a psychological sense there are revelations but very often they're false ones. It happens to characters in my books that they have revelations which can't be followed up. There's one in *The Unicorn*. People sometimes feel that they've had a sudden vision of good, or of a better life, or spiritual reality or something. But this may be just a psychological freak or it may be something which is based on what is good but which they can't grasp. To put it again in terms of a Platonic image, there could be flashes from a higher level which you can't actually make anything of because your own level is so low. You can't grasp this as a reality, as something that makes a real difference to your life. If the test of revelation is in terms of its making a difference, and there is no difference because you can't see how to use it or what it leads to, what is its value? I know people do often say, 'I had a revelation at a certain time' or 'I felt I had been visited by God' or 'This has made a difference to me ever after; I've always thought about it when I was in difficulties' and so on, and I think this can happen: the 'flash' from the higher level which they might feel was a kind of permanent possession and a guiding light. But I have not experienced this myself.

Yet it seems hard for me to understand that you can write so powerfully without having experienced something similar yourself.

Well, I think any artist makes for a revelation. To use

Freudian terminology which has become part of our ordinary speech, I think that there certainly is such a thing as the unconscious mind. There are these extraordinary deep reservoirs of imagery and thought and force: great power, darkness and terror which are in the mind and the soul and sometimes you get a kind of energy which comes from this region, some unexpected enlightenment or vision. Or again, the sort of thing that people use the word 'grace' to mean; that you suddenly find that you can do something which you didn't think you could do, and people might say, 'God helped you at that moment'. Well, I think in art one often has these feelings, and you can get them from your own art and from great art.

These are ambiguous things because they're very often connected with sex. For example, in the case of Tom in my novel *The Philosopher's Pupil* I think it was a great sexual revelation that Tom received, a kind of earth force. Yet later on he might make something of remembering that experience and see it as a spiritual thing, like a moral ordeal. This is how the mind is so odd, that it uses these ambiguous things. The erotic aspect of our lives is deeply connected with the spiritual. There are great winds that blow from another place which give you strength or make you feel that you understand. You can see this as something erotic or you can see it as something spritual.

When Dora in The Bell *goes into the art gallery and has some sort of revelatory experience as she stands in front of a Gainsborough, what was passing between that painting and Dora?*

The painting in question is of two children with a butterfly. Dora has a butterfly experience too and there's something childish about her. But there's also what was happening in the mind of the writer. I think this is a marvellous picture. It's a very 'painterly' picture, the sort of picture that a painter would be interested in. Now Dora's a painter and a child, and somehow it was right, I thought, for her to be looking at this picture. It has a kind of simplicity about it which is moving. In trying to describe such an experience one can use all sorts of ordinary words like, 'All my anxieties fell away and I realised that what I was worrying about was not worth worrying about!' All the things that nag away at one, the fantasies of power or of revenge; anxiety, resentment and envy — all of this is what the revelation will blot out. And it will prove that they can be blotted out.

I think that there is an element of proof involved in these truths. I would think the word 'truth' is in place, the discovery of truth, is the discovery of good, and this may be an experience of revelation. You realise, or you suddenly see, the lies and the falsity in the pictures which you've been building up. This kind of egoistic anxiety, this cloud of cobwebs can be swept away by an experience of art or an experience of nature, an experience of talking to somebody or seeing somebody working.

We've been talking so far about Dora. Has this sort of experience ever happened to you?

Yes. The two arts that I'm very close to are literature and painting. I wanted very much to be a painter. I'm very moved by painting. I think I said earlier that I believe the word revelation is ambiguous and whether it means anything in the long-term can always be doubtful. But I think one can have extraordinary feelings of exaltation and, to come back to the word 'truth', the feeling that your own shadowy ideas, your cobweb of anxieties and so on, is parted like a curtain, and you look into a world created by some great genius, himself inspired by forces beyond. Suddenly, it's an image of the death of egoism. Religion is about the death of the ego. The ego disappears and you see the world with absolute vividness and clarity.

I felt this when I saw the picture by Titian in the Venice Exhibition, 'The Flaying of Marsyas'. It's a huge extraordinary picture which lives in Czechoslovakia. People said what a cruel picture it is: 'How awful, Apollo flaying Marsyas!' but without going into the iconography, this clearly had a significance for the people of the Renaissance as an image of the death of the self — that the god flays you, that you lose your egoism in this sort of agony, which is also ecstacy. The expression on the face of Marsyas is ecstatic. The beauty and intensity of the picture — it's a wonderful picture, painted by Titian when, I think, he was over ninety. It was a sense of the burning of the human spirit in front of one's eyes. I feel the same way about Shakespeare. How can a human being do such a great thing? It's full of imaginative resonance and spiritual resonance: one lives, one can live on such things.

Leaving aside your admiration for the artistry of the creator of the picture, what actually happened to you as you stood in front of that picture?

Well, I was completely stunned. I didn't know this picture existed. I've seen a great many Titians in different places and I'd never heard of this one. I just went into that room and there it was.

It's also a subject that interests me. I've thought a lot about the 'Flaying of Marsyas', as a sort of icon, a religious icon. In the picture Apollo is kneeling and very lovingly removing the skin. A figure, perhaps a satyr, is helping him, and another satyr is so touchingly bringing a heavy bucket of water in a humble way, like a servant. They have become servants of Apollo. And then there's a child, there are two dogs and a very beautiful fiddler who's looking upwards with a rapt expression. There's a lovely luminous brown light in the picture, I think it's dawn, they're settling down to a long job. Then there is Midas, sitting on the right, who was connected with judging the contest between Marsyas and Apollo. The story is that Marsyas said he was as good a musician as Apollo. Unfortunately he did not win. Midas is sitting in a sad, pensive attitude, looking at it all. He is like us, a spectator. The intensity of the whole picture is so great, it conveys a deep symbolic impression of human life with all its ambiguity, all its horrors and terrors and miseries — yet, at the same time, it's joyful and beautiful. It is to do with the entry of the spiritual into the human situation and the closeness of the gods.

Did that moment change you at all?

Oh, I don't know. It influences a lot of things connected with art for me. It's the sort of picture which enters into my work, and it's the greatest experience of that kind I've ever had. No, I shouldn't think it has changed me — I wish it had or may.

Iris Murdoch, thank you very much.

DOUG SCOTT

DOUG SCOTT was born in 1941 in Nottingham. He
began climbing at the age of twelve and has become one of
Britain's best known mountaineers. He reached the summit
of Mount Everest with Dougal Haston in 1975, via the
south-west face and has an impressive list of 'firsts' on
mountains and rock faces throughout the world. He became
the President of the Alpine Climbing Group in 1976; he
lectures internationally and published *Big Wall Climbing* in
1974. More recently with Alex MacIntyre, he published
Shishapangna Tibet. He lives quietly with his wife and
family in the Lake District where he pursues his interest in
the spiritual aspects of man's nature.

Interviewed by Eric Robson

I can imagine that there is a mysterious communion between climbers and their mountains. What is the force that pushes you on to the mountains and keeps you going even in the most trying circumstances?

For anybody that's got a job in the city, to get out at weekends is just so good. Spending a weekend rock climbing and camping in the Peak or Lake District, or any mountain area, is just good therapy.

Is it the thrill that drives you on though?

That's part of it. And also the adrenalin rush. A month ago we were on Makalu, we set off at the bottom of this six mile ridge. The three of us were becoming more cut off the higher we got. We actually had to go up the ridge and down into a basin: it was like putting your neck into a noose. And then we had to climb the head wall. Now if we couldn't go over the top and down the easy way we were really in trouble. Suddenly we were in that trouble because one of the lads fell ill and we had to come back the hard way. That was all at 27,000 feet; so what was going to take 5 days, took 9 days and we were really quite exhausted by the end of it. I mean, I really wondered if we had the energy to come down this head wall and then climb up again a thousand feet to get back down the ridge. And that was quite exciting at the time.

So it's pushing yourself to the limit?

In that case yes: it really drained me from my stomach and it took me a few weeks to recover. It was just like the life force had been depleted from that one, because so many times you had to put yourself back on your feet and start breaking trail again. And then you would collapse exhausted; I mean all you wanted to do really was to carry on staying there and to go to sleep. Mind you we had a bit of a scare near the summit of Makalu; we came across this chap that had sat down in

1978 for a rest. His two companions had gone further down and we found him there frozen onto the rocks. He just sat there as if he was sitting in his armchair and I think that was good for us, in that it reminded us what happens if you do sit down and shut your eyes when you are really exhausted, as totally exhausted as we were.

You have come close to death several times and a lot of your friends have died in those mountains. One particular case was your close friend, Nick Escort. Can you tell me what happened there and what the effect of that accident was on you?

Well it was right out of the blue. Nick and I were just shuttling gear across a snow slope to the top camp. We were stocking a camp higher up which had been cut off for three days in a storm. I went across towing eight hundred feet of rope. Nick and I were clipped onto a rope in the centre of a snow slope when the whole thing avalanched. All I had time to do was see Nick going over and the ice and snow breaking up and plunging towards these 4,000 foot cliffs. Then a jolt came onto me as this eight hundred foot rope came tight. There's a lot of elasticity in nylon. I was just catapulted down head over heels, heading towards the big drop and, as I went, I remember thinking, 'Well this is it. So this is what it is like to be in an avalanche.' I had visions of snow and rocks rushing by and also I had this certain feeling, 'Well I'm now going to die but it wouldn't be a bad thing!' A warm feeling came over me. This was all in a few seconds, hurtling downhill. Then I stopped dead in the snow. I'd got a lot of weight on my back, about 65 lbs. and the rope snapped. I was left on the edge to see the snow and ice and Nick plunge down. I had to scramble up to the camp and eventually get back down to base. But that did leave me with something. When it sank in, after a few weeks, I had this kind of confidence in myself. Mainly because from there on I realised I wasn't afraid to die: it wouldn't be a bad thing to happen. It's hard to describe it really but that's the effect it had on me. I didn't want to die and I don't want to die now, but I'm not afraid to die. The big problem of course, is the people you leave behind and I've seen enough of that not to want to risk myself: to put myself into ridiculously risky situations.

And yet you do that time and time again, don't you? I mean you've been involved in an accident at 24,000 feet, broke both your legs and somehow got down the mountain. How did you manage to summon up the reserves of energy, stamina and will power to get down that mountain?

Well, I think anyone that's fit enough to be up there and that wants to get home badly enough, would find ways to do it. On that occasion I was a bit daft. Chris Bonington and I had just been to the summit of the Ogre in Pakistan. It was late at night and the sun had set. I was anxious to get down about 2,000 feet to where the other lads and our sleeping bags were in a snow cave. So I made the first abseil from the summit, threw the ropes down and slid down them. But we had left some gear lower down and I was having to tension across some slabs to pick it up and then carry on. But that evening it was very cold and the water that had melted from the snow along the rocks had frozen to verglas and I inadvertently stood on this verglas. As I tensioned off, my legs went from under me and I was away on a huge 'Tarzan' swing across this gulley and smashed into the rocks on the other side and was left dangling on the end of the rope. I managed to get on to a little ledge or, at least, half my backside on to a ledge and put a peg in and I clipped on to it. As I was doing this, I realised there was a strange crackling noise in my ankles. Chris Bonington came down over the overhang and arranged the abseils down to a little bivouac ledge which we cut out of the ice. We spent the night there. The next day I crawled and Chris climbed down to the

other lads, Mo Anthoine and Clive Rowlands. Then we
had a storm for five days and we went without food for four
of them. It was eight days before we actually got down to
base camp. There were three days on a stretcher for me and
Chris was hobbling on at my side because he'd broken his
ribs on the way down. So it was quite an epic all round! But
I didn't think then that 'This was it'. I always felt that with
those lads, and my own reserves, it was possible to get
down.

*After the death of another very close friend, Dougal Haston, you
had what you've described as a spiritual experience.*

Well, Dougal had a girl friend who was suffering enormous
grief by his death. They had such a close relationship and
she said that half of herself had died with Dougal. Anyway,
she was in such a bad way she ended up by staying with my
family for quite some time. She was having a real hard time
of it. She would go out with me when I lectured. I was
writing a book on Everest and I was visiting all the climbers
that had been to Everest. I had just been to see Tilman and
we were motoring back home through Wales. Suddenly,
the whole landscape became very vibrant and there were
streams of energy on the periphery of my vision, all zapping
around. The intensity of that experience, the sort of
vibrancy in the scenery and everything, was for just a few
seconds but I was left feeling quite different. I certainly had
a lot more compassion than ever I had had before. Not that I
had a lot but, after that, for a week or two, perhaps a few
months, I could understand people's problems. I could see
the unity of everything, if you like. How everything was
connected. I could make all kinds of connections I had never
been able to do before. But it's hard to describe. It was just a
very heightened perception — but as I say, it only lasted for
a few seconds at a real intensity but I had a different outlook

on life from then on. Very strongly for a few weeks; months afterwards, it had lost its intensity.

In what way was this new compassion, this new unity showing itself?

I would somehow get involved with friends and acquaintances who had various problems, whereas before I was kind of quite ineffective. At that time I was effective in helping them with the problems and with support, sympathy, understanding and awareness. It's a bit too personal to talk about really but it did significantly change my direction and I still don't know quite why it happened. But I think, perhaps for the first time, I was doing something for someone else without expecting any reward. For example, totally putting myself out for this lass, really just listening to her going through her grieving, helping her through it by just listening to what she had got to say about her relationship; she being so emphatic that she wanted someone to understand where they had been; what level they had reached in their relationship.

Before this lass came to stay with us, I had been working on myself to some extent, because I was writing this Everest book and I was looking at myself to question my motives as to why I climb. Being with these old timers, I was trying to weigh up why they did certain things on the mountain: but I was really examining myself, my motives. So I had been doing some work on myself. I mean, trying to be as honest as I could be and realising a lot of my own defects. Then she made me work hard to understand where she had been to along the path. It had lifted me up to a new way of looking at the whole business of being alive. Whether it was work on myself or just doing something for someone else without expecting anything back, I don't know, but suddenly I got everything back.

Did you ever make any other kind of connection at the time?

Well, after this experience, I did get interested in literature on this topic and it's only the last year or two that I've calmed myself down a bit because it was so profound for me. I wondered what it was and I wanted confirmation. I started reading avidly, all kinds of esoteric literature, Tao, I Ching and a lot more besides.

Has this experience had a lasting effect on you?

Well, very strongly for two or three months, but it is still more than just a memory, it's a reference point. When I find myself in a quagmire again, bogged down with too much to do and not doing any of it well, it's good for me to remind myself where I can be at that level.

So, you don't feel you've lost it altogether?

No. It's always there but it's not right in the front. At first I thought this was it. I thought: 'This is me, now I'm up here and I don't have to work at it or do anything.' That's very wrong. When it happens, you can easily make a fool of yourself, you can get carried away with it, you can indulge in it. It can be very confusing for your friends and acquaintances when suddenly, there's me, an average sort of chap suddenly turning up at base camp with a whole stack of esoteric literature and raving on about it and saying: 'Why can't you see this, and that?' It was all so obvious to me, but very few people knew what I was going on about.

It seems that there are parallels between what you've been talking about and very intense religious experiences. In the story of you coming down from the mountain with the broken legs, you put yourself through pain and suffering over a long period of time. Is it a parallel with religious asceticism?

Well, that's part of climbing although it's not part of this particular experience. What happened to me was not on a mountain. Nothing like that happened after reaching the top of Everest. But I suppose what you are talking about does happen. You do take on the role of an ascetic while you are on the mountain: not self-flagellation exactly but your hands are all beaten up, especially after five days on a vertical granite rock face and you deny yourself sleep. You don't sleep or eat much on the mountain and that might be a key to the heightened sensory perception. In 1980, I had been on Makalu for nine days with Roger Baxter-Jones and George Bettembourg and we really did push ourselves to the limit. Afterwards, at base camp, it was so peaceful. I felt relaxed in myself and so at peace with everyone around me. The internal dialogue, that rush of thoughts, well, I could pick them off one at a time. You could feel the thoughts coming: there was a space between the thoughts. In that space there was calm and peace. I am not in that space now at this moment, but the experience is a reference point. I value it.

Do you find this often when you've done a difficult climb? For example, when you get to the top of a climb and perhaps due to lack of oxygen, perhaps just sheer exhaustion, or physical effort, do you see things in a different perspective?

Well, through your senses, yes. And there's this calmness, it might even be confidence, in that you've achieved your ambition — just like anything. I mean, you don't have to go off to the mountains to do this, in fact, it's probably a very silly and expensive way of going about it — I'm sure you can do it all in your back garden if you had the technique and the real burning desire like so many people do. You keep coming across them. But this just happens to be the way I've gone and what's happened on the side has proved to be more beneficial than actually reaching any summits. There are things that happened to me during my climbing which I never expected and which are now part of me — built into my being which can't be taken away from me, can't be lost. But I keep going after summits, you can never really satisfy that; the ambition to be on the top all the time. All you can do is keep doing more of it.

But having experienced that wonderful moment of spiritual revelation we were talking about before, do you hope that you will have one of those moments of revelation again?

I daren't even hope for it — if it happens great, but you know if you try too hard you won't. It's the same with trying to achieve anything. In mountaineering *wanting* so much to achieve a summit doesn't seem to be the way of going about it, it's almost when I let go of my ambition to climb a peak that events have often worked to allow me to get there. The weather's improved, somebody's health has improved, and we've gone up and it's worked out beautifully but with some humility that time. But when I've gone full pelt, determined and 'I can do it', that's when I ended up with two broken legs.

So you're not going to try too hard to recapture your revelation, just hope it will happen to you?

Yes.

Doug Scott, thank you very much indeed.

POSTSCRIPT

I left the studio agreeing with my wife, Jan, that the interview had gone well because for once, the interviewer had given me the opportunity to consider my replies. But my mind was full of what I had not managed to say. I felt I had conveyed only a small part of the experience. That revelation, whilst unexpected, was not a total surprise — the text of it was somehow familiar. Physically I did have an actual taste in the back of my mouth for weeks afterwards; I felt in control of my body to such an extent that I could heal myself. I could sense other people's needs wherever I met them just by becoming calm, relaxed, interested and sympathetic to them.

I have subsequently studied Ouspensky and his theory that most of us are asleep and Gurdjieff's teaching that most of us live in a state of sleep. It has come as quite a shock realising that much of the time I am asleep, then waking up to hidden faults within me. There's no doubt I woke up in Wales. I had a glimpse of the vast potential that is there for me and for all of us: it would have been a harder life without it.

PAUL TORTELIER

PAUL TORTELIER was born in Paris in 1914 to a poor artisan family and showed his musical talents at an early age. Supported by his Breton mother, he was playing with major orchestras in his early twenties and his international reputation was established with Sir Thomas Beecham in 1947. A political idealist, he almost abandoned his career in favour of living on a kibbutz but returned to a grateful public and, supported by his wife, has toured throughout the world including Russia, America, Japan and China. His own compositions, dedicated to the cause of international peace, include songs and music for cello and orchestra. He is happily married with four children yet he maintains an intensely busy concert schedule and is eager to bring his music to the widest possible audience by playing in small provincial concerts as well as international centres.
Interviewed by Eric Robson

When you are playing music do you experience a mystical link with the composer?

Yes. We are part of a chain but we never know exactly what emerges from our playing. When I play the Dvorak Cello Concerto I know that Dvorak had been thinking of his friend. I know it. So there are things that you know and there are things that you have been told. It is difficult to pretend that it is completely mystical.

But when you are playing, when you are interpreting a piece of music is there a process of revelation?

Certainly there is. It is also there when you compose. An idea comes to you, but from where does it come? From where? But there is another revelation. My mother and father discovered music as simple workers — my father was a cabinet maker and they were not musical. The revelation was really from them. My father discovered the beauty of the Pastoral Symphony and the Ninth Symphony. This met his ideals and this has been conveyed in my blood. I feel the same love for the Pastoral Symphony for instance because of my love of nature. It is all these threads coming together in my life that makes my revelation. It is not something just like a flash, it is a slow process.

Is there a particular piece of music or a concert, when you felt the power of revelation being imparted to you more strongly?

I was a teenager when I heard Wagner's Siegfried Idyll. I really cried. I couldn't help crying, so beautiful it was. I probably had plenty of love in my heart but I didn't know at that time. It was, perhaps, a revelation to make me understand what love is. The famous Auguste Rodin has written a book, *The Cathedrals of France*, in which he says that an artist is somebody who is lucky enough to be in love. I was in love from the very beginning. I was in love with life, with games, sport, music and nature; with everything in life. Progressively music taught me that everything is love. And when I play this Dvorak, I play it well because I am in love with Dvorak.

People go to church and kneel in front of the Virgin, and I, each time I play works by Beethoven and Bach and the other great composers, I kneel in front of Angels.

So you describe and experience music as the very language of love?

Yes, but there are so many loves. Chopin expresses the love of women; Schubert and Debussy express the love of nature; Beethoven expressed the love of mankind; Bach the love of God and also the love of family. Bach's family was a fantastic family. He had twenty children. The two Bourrées from the 3rd Suite for Cello, one in C major and one in C minor, are about his family. In my imagination — and imagination is so important to an artist — Bach is dancing with his children. In a moment of real happiness he forgets all his problems in life and he dances with the children. But in the C minor Bourrée I think of the sadness in the man because so many of his children passed away.

Do you use music in the same way an Eastern mystic might try to find himself or might try to find an explanation for the world through mystical contact with a spiritual dimension?

Perhaps the reality of music is to make silence sing, to make the silence sing. And the mystics of the Eastern countries, they care very much for silence for their meditation.

It is important to speak about silence. I have the impression that some music is almost silent, it is so high, so detached from our materialistic world. Music is the least materialistic art. The Saraband in C minor from the 5th Suite for Cello by Bach, is a prayer and a meditation. It lives in silence. By the way, I know few works of music so pure and so economical in sounds. When I play this piece in public, nobody dares to applaud. It seems to start from silence and come back to silence. An extension of silence. Silence is peace. Silence is serenity.

It is a great pity that people are afraid of silence today. It shows how unhappy they are inside. They always need music; music that is not music, music that is not part of silence, music that is a drug. They can't do without this noise. I want to tell you something more. There is another piece, by Handel, which I play with my wife, the third movement of his Sonata for two Cellos (transcribed from the Sonata for two Violins). It is beautiful and once, after we had played it in a church in France, a lady came to us and I shall never forget what she said, 'Thank you very much, Madame and Monsieur Tortelier. I wish I had heard this piece of Handel twenty years ago when I lost my daughter. It would have helped me so much.'

But has music ever become a drug for you?

Perhaps music is a need which you can consider like a consolation for your physical and mental balance. You know, when you are surrounded by music you don't know if you need it. When I play a vivacious piece of music by Bach, it has the same virtue as a shower — for the last six months, I have taken cold showers and I've discovered that they give me a good start to the day. An old man of nearly ninety years said to me, 'My secret is a cold shower.' Sometimes when I play, it is like swimming in the ocean. In this case, perhaps it is a sort of drug. I am not sure.

Well, is there a parallel between your music and religion?

Ah! Alors! That is more a positive question! I'm not sure that people have noticed the significance of polyphonic music. Polyphonic music is made by a group of four people. It allows these four people to unite in beauty and to talk together with sounds. I say to 'talk together with sounds' because it is impossible to talk in this way with words. If you imagine four people talking together, especially if one is speaking Chinese, another Russian, a third German and a fourth French, the result will be chaos. This shows that there is something extraordinary in music and I think it should be considered as a new religion.

This has not been recognised because this phenomenon happened only a short time ago. How long since people have sung like this? Four centuries only since Europe discovered this religion, while the religions which are based on words, Judaism, the Christian religion, the Hindu and Buddhist religions, were made thousands of years ago. Now my idea is that this new musical religion has to be spread for the benefit of mankind. I respect the traditional religions but they are not a complete success. One reason for this, is that you have to translate the Gospels from Hebrew to French or to English, and it changes the meaning and sometimes the words become dangerous because they divide us.

I am interested in this point you're making about the oneness of music, the unifying force in music which runs throughout the world. Do you believe that there is any contact with any divine being through music?

The problem with religion is that we are taught differently. Somebody will be taught about a certain God and somebody else will be taught about another God. You will tell me it is the same God but these people will still have wars. They say their God speaks differently to them. The God of the Iranians says, 'Attack this man who doesn't think like you.' The Christian God says, 'If you receive anything you must turn the other cheek.' The Jewish God says, 'An eye for an eye, a tooth for a tooth.'

Music will never do this. The message of Bach, of

Beethoven and Mozart, can only be a blessing. Some call it humanitarian. I call it divine. In the old religions Paradise is a promise; you don't know that you are going to Paradise, it's just a promise. But with Bach, the Paradise is brought down to earth. For me, it's enough!

Let's forget about believing, that is a matter of education and you cannot have everybody educated the same way, all over the world. But music speaks to the Chinese without translation. When I speak to the Chinese with Beethoven they laugh with me, they cry with me — we kiss each other.

Do you think that the revelation which is music, points a way to the truth?

I think harmony is the truth. In harmony there is also beauty and love. That is truth. Harmony is the key point of the Christian religion and, I think, of other religions too. Now religion speaks about love and speaks about harmony, but music, when you find the religion of music, it acts love and acts harmony. It is a direct activity of love. I hope this is clear!

I recently played the Dvorak Concerto in Liverpool. Everybody thought something was special. And you know why, because suddenly I realised it was the birthday of my wife, my dear wife, with whom I am never, so I had to call her. There was a telephone there in the artistes' room and I telephoned to her but she was not home. I couldn't join her to wish her 'Happy Birthday'.

Then I went to the stage and I played Dvorak. For the first time I didn't care about any dangerous shifting, any dangerous problem, for you know, nothing is more difficult than to play a string instrument. Everything went well, but what is true, is that from beginning to end I was in thought with my wife. The performance was dedicated to her. I've never played the Dvorak Concerto like that, in my whole life. The musicians felt something happened, the public felt something happened. I explained to them afterwards and I said, 'That's why I played like that tonight.' Now love was present there at the performance, pure love. Excuse me to confess this to you, but it must be emphasized that love is the very thing for an artist. You have the proof.

Is your mission in life to pass on that love, that way to the truth, to the people who listen to your music?

Yes. Yes, it's a mission. We musicians are missionaries. We are re-creators and olympic winners because it's a sport; we are painters because music has plenty of colour to produce, we are architects, if music is not built it falls into pieces and it doesn't catch the attention of the listener. We are also a priest because we convey the message of gods who died three hundred years ago. It is a great responsibility, to be sure that we do not betray them. We are like Christ — we resurrect — we make a resurrection.

When I play Schubert, I feel as unhappy as he was. My imagination works, I am with him. People say, 'What are you thinking about when you play?' I think about the one I love and the one I love is Schubert, if I play Schubert. If I pass from one to another, I go to my wife, or to my mother or to the public. Of course, it's communion through me. But I cannot think of the public as such because the public are a few thousand people and for me they have to become one. The thing is to make them one. I cannot play for two different people. I have to have a centre. We all need a centre — so my centre is Schubert or my wife, or my little ones. But the people, they are always with me, in communion with my mind.

But through that communion, are you trying to give those people who are listening to you, a similar revelation?

I am not too intellectual — I just want to bring them joy. The religion of my father was the religion of Beethoven, it was joy. When we speak of love we speak of joy because if you love you find a double joy. You have the joy for yourself and you have the joy for the one you love, because it is a gift. It's not just to say, 'I love you': it's to give the proof. It is to bring something to the beloved. Now this gives you a double joy. Beethoven's religion was a joy. He said, 'A pure day of joy in the temple of nature and mankind.' That's why he wrote the Ninth Symphony, joy for the world. And that's what I want to bring to the audience.

Paul Tortelier – thank you very much.

SIR LAURENS
VAN DER POST

SIR LAURENS VAN DER POST was born in 1906 in
Philippolis, the Orange Free State, South Africa. He left
home in his late teens to pursue a career in journalism and
travelled widely, finally settling in London. He spent the
early years of the war fighting behind enemy lines in North
Africa and Java where he was captured by the Japanese. In
1947 he was awarded the C.B.E. and was knighted in 1981.
His meeting with the late Lord Mountbatten and Carl
Jung has served him well to bring a significant contribution
to the life and literature of this nation. He has written over
twenty books including, *Venture to the Interior* (Amy Woolf
Memorial Prize), *The Lost World of the Kalahari* (American
Literary Guild Choice) both of which celebrate the wisdom
of his beloved Africa. He has also made several films
including *The Story of Carl Gustav Jung*.
Interviewed by Eric Robson

Sir Laurens, I think that people are pretty certain what the material world is, but equally I think that some people are on rather shakier ground when it comes to describing the spiritual world. You're particularly good at describing the impact of the spiritual world in your books: what impact does that spiritual world have on you?

Gosh, you start me off in very great difficulty. I'm not certain that I see all that much of a distinction between the material and the spiritual world. In a way I have a feeling that what we call the material world is reality seen from without and, what we call the spiritual world, is reality seen from within.

That goes back to what I imagine is one of the greatest misconceptions of our time. People think that what we experience within ourselves is subjective and what we experience without is objective. They don't realise that we have within us an enormous objective world. The spirit is primarily concerned with that inner objectivity. But really one can't describe, and I don't think anybody has succeeded in describing in rational terms, what the spiritual is. I go to your key word, 'impact': we ultimately know reality indirectly through the impact it has on us. We can see the spiritual urges that have swept through mankind; that have raised cathedrals; that have induced man to be an artist, to create beyond himself; that have created poetry; created music; made man cross the oceans and now go out into outer space. These are consequences of the spirit. The spirit is that which gives man a meaning but we only know it through the impact it makes.

And when I've said all these things I've said to you, it's something more — one really has to express it symbolically. What has been the great image of the spirit, with primitive people and with modern people, is the wind. It's the wind that moves. Nobody knows where it comes from or where it's going to but it moves us. The first people of Africa I

115

knew — you should have heard them talk about the wind. The sort of pneumanistic tone that comes into their voices about the wind, the wind of the spirit. Take the great French poet, Valéry, who wrote that very great poem, 'The Graveyard of the Sailors', the last lines of which are: 'The wind rises, the spirit moves and one must try to live.' It's that which makes us live a life of meaning.

Can you remember the first time in your life when this wind of the spirit actually touched you, when you had your first revelation?

Well — I'm not side-stepping — it's very difficult because revelation hasn't been a sudden process for me. It seems to me, looking back, that one's whole life, has been a continuing process of revelation and there are certain moments when the process of revelation builds up rather like a thundercloud: builds up out of imponderables in the atmosphere. And suddenly there's a discharge of lightning. But it's a slow continuing process and, to me, the astounding thing and the most lovely thing about life, is that it's been a sustained process, which gets more and more intense as one has grown older. But it has unpredictable things to it. I always say I hesitate to take my imagination and mind beyond the natural walls, but the most extraordinary things come over the walls to one, that simply can't be ignored, can't be explained rationally.

As a child, I had an experience which I've never forgotten. I don't know what it means to this day but it seems to me to have something to do with revelation. One day I was out alone with my gun in a rather dangerous part of Africa where we were living. It was a lovely blue, Spring morning and I had promised I would get a couple of wild birds for lunch. I had promised I would cook them. I was very young at the time — about eight — but I could shoot. I went out and I got about a mile from the homestead on this shining morning, when there was the most incredible flash of lightning and I was filled with fear. I turned round and ran back home. I knew what a bolt from the blue meant. It's that flash of lightning, which is greater than the light of day, that in a way has been a compass to me, but I can't say any more about it than that.

Do you know what it was telling you? Have you any ideas?

Well, it was telling me that there was another light, there was an instantaneous, a spontaneous light that was peculiarly my own. It couldn't have come out of the blue like that. It was something more. As I grew older it was inside myself, there was lightning within me that I had to follow, just as animals in Africa, in a period of drought when the rains are about to break, see flashes of lightning far, far below the horizon and they make for it. I had a flash of lightning in a period of drought that I had to make for.

Have these flashes of lightning happened to you throughout your life? Do they happen regularly?

Well, things have happened to me that have made me think about this original flash of lightning. I don't quite know yet what it was. Suddenly I find myself doing things, as it were, by lightning. I've suddenly found myself doing things which I hadn't premeditated. Usually in moments of great danger or great crisis, there has been this sort of instantaneous thing that's made me take a leap into the dark of myself.

On reading your books it struck me that so many of these things happened in moments of crisis, moments of danger. Why do you think they should happen at moments of danger like that?

I think they happen because we bring with us into life all the experience of life that there has ever been. If you think how short our own span of life is, how little we add to the knowing that we bring with us. In a sense, to me, living is getting to know again; a remembering in a contemporary way, of the knowledge that we bring into life with us.

A sort of reincarnation? Or would that be too simple a way of putting it?

No. It's a remembrance. I think the whole of life is a re-remembrance, in a contemporary way, of all that life has taught people who have lived life in the past, and built into this knowledge the experience we bring into life with us. There are means of dealing with a kind of crisis that come to us like lightning. That's why, in moments of crisis particularly, it's almost as if another person or a voice takes one over. I can remember quite a simple example of it.

We were in a Japanese prison at a very critical period when we were really living from day to day; a sort of side by side with death. One didn't know whether you would live through the next day or not; whether you might not be executed. We had a terrible crisis and were very weak and very ill. We all had to parade and the Japanese wanted us to do something which I felt I couldn't agree to tell my men to do, as an officer.

They lined us up and began beating up people while they were posting machine guns all round the parade ground. From previous experiences I had had, I knew this was going to lead to a killing and I was not going to be able to stop it. The Japanese were calling out the officers one by one and as they came out they were beating them down. When my turn came, I walked out and a Japanese Warrant Officer knocked me down completely; it was a tremendous crack! I stood up and he sort of shooed me away and I turned to go. Then a voice inside me suddenly said to me, 'Go back and let him beat you again!' Instantly I turned round and walked back. As I stood in front of him, he raised a chair high above his head, a wooden chair in which he had been sitting and, as he did so, he suddenly thought, 'but I've just knocked this man down.'

It started off something else in him — I'd broken the rhythm of something evil without my knowing it and he kicked me, threw the chair away and walked away in disgust. The whole situation collapsed. Now, I'm quite certain if I hadn't done that, a lot of people would have been killed that day, but I had no knowledge that I was going to do it. That is one small example.

You've described yourself in Who's Who *as a Christian – do you think that voice was God talking to you?*

Did I describe myself as that? It's a very big claim. I couldn't possibly describe myself in any other way, in the sense that if I have to present a category of the spirit of mankind with which I identify, it is with a Christian Western civilisation culture. But I mustn't overdo the description.

So when you heard the voice saying 'go back', could that have been the voice of your God talking to you?

I thought of it as the voice of creation, of life. I've always felt, and my experience has proved it, that there's something in us, whether we die or not, which is always just a jump ahead of death. And it was the voice of creation, I feel, speaking at that moment.

If I could speak with a scientific voice for a moment. Could a scientist not say to you that the mind has a safety mechanism which it switches on at that particular moment rather in the way that the body creates natural opiates in times of pain?

Well, I know that scientists tend to do that and I think, when they do, they fail their own calling. They forget that, as Einstein put it, 'The spirit of science is devout', and that science has tended to reduce the spirit to a process of rationalism. The spirit is not just rationalism. Reason is part of the spirit: it is one of the instruments of the spirit. Reason is the master passion of mankind, and it's one of the most terrible things about our age that we've allowed what was a passion of the spirit, to decline into an arid form of intellectualism.

Let's set aside the scientific voice. Speaking personally, I don't remember ever having had one of those flashes of lightning – is that a failing in me?

No, I don't see why you should. It comes to us in so many different ways. In any of the great experiences of the spirit, the great traditions of religion, it's fantastic the diverse ways in which it speaks to different people. It can just speak through a woman, a despised woman, who suddenly knelt down and washed Christ's feet. That was a form of revelation. It couldn't come to her rationally but she acted it out. It's a great failing to ignore the many voices in which the one voice of the spirit speaks to mankind.

Is it possible then, do you think, for all of us to open ourselves, to make ourselves receptive to revelation?

I do think so. One of the great failures of our time is that we appear to have lost our direction to the ways in which we can have a revelation of this sort: this overall drive which is in every human being. I think we all know far more than our upbringing and the conventions and fashions of the intellect and the mind allow us to acknowledge. We can all break through that in simple ways. And I think it's a beginning because always there is something in life which tries to compensate, if life goes too far in one direction. I think people are beginning to realise that the spirit and the meaning is not purely a rational process. I'm not belittling reason, because it's marvellous, but I'm terrified of the extent to which reason has become a form of hubris — it has exceeded its own proportions, it has exceeded it's place in the totality of the human spirit. There are so many non-rational ways in which the spirit comes into us. I've mentioned the artist: you can't explain the artist rationally; you can't explain the priest or the composer rationally; you can't explain the scientist rationally; what is it that drives him? What was it that made Archimedes suddenly realise that the water he displaced in a bath was the measurement of his own body? What was it that made Euclid suddenly take these abstract images that occurred to him and explore them scientifically? What was it that made the great maxims of mathematics on which our world, our physics and everything is founded today, the great religious statements that they are? You see these things are non-rational images that come to us, we don't think them. One of the most appalling things that ever happened was that people believed Descartes' statement, 'I think: therefore I am', because really there is something thinking through us. The Germans have a great word for it, they call it 'einfall' — an inspiration — that falls into us suddenly, a flash of lightning, and a thought we didn't even know we had, is recognised. Revelation is an act of recognition — a flashing act of recognition, a re-remembering of a great knowledge in contemporary life and terms which has always been there.

We've been talking about the failures of 1984 man and the barriers he has put up, but perhaps people listening to this conversation will say, 'It is easier for Laurens van der Post to have these moments of revelation; he goes to exotic places; he can stand in the middle of the Bush and be closer to his creator. It's rather more difficult for me, because I'm on Social Security in Barrow-in-Furness and all I see is a 38 bus going past the window three or four times a day.' Is it not more difficult for someone in that latter situation?

I think it's always difficult — I think it can be difficult in the

Bush too — but the things I have been talking about, haven't happened to me in the Bush only. I've talked to you about what happened in a Japanese Prisoner of War Camp and in other places.

What is interesting to me is that life has never been more secure than it is at the moment. Shakespeare was an old man at fifty and I don't feel all that old at the age of over seventy. Life has become longer, life is much more secure. A man on Social Security is living a life of incredible luxury compared with the man of the past. The key word is security, and yet, spiritually, in the sense I've been talking about, man has never felt more threatened and insecure. He has never been more frightened. Look at this terrible fear of the atom bomb. Look at these forces that we ourselves have created and given ourselves; we don't know how to control them. And because of this imbalance, we've never felt more insecure.

But if you think of the moments of crisis as having great value, if you think of the way the old Chinese sages thought of it — so much so that the Chinese idiogram for crisis and opportunity are the same — perhaps we have crises so that we can experience this other thing in ourselves. We now have leisure which, used positively, could also provide an opportunity to get to know ourselves; to find out what we are about inside ourselves. I think we have a great opportunity to experience the kind of revelation that we've been talking about. It is continuous, I don't think it always needs to be dramatic. I have much more belief and faith in evolutionary revelation than these very startling and dramatic ones, important as they are.

Sir Laurens van der Post, thank you very much.

KENNETH WILLIAMS

KENNETH WILLIAMS, actor and comedian, was born in London in 1926 and trained as a lithograph draughtsman. As a National Serviceman he enlisted in the Army and was posted to Ceylon (Sri Lanka) where the events described in this interview took place.

He subsequently joined a repertory company and was soon starring with Kenneth Horne, Tony Hancock and, of course, was a bastion of the *Carry On* film series. But it was in the BBC Radio series *Just a Minute*, in cameo descriptions of classical history and literature, that he demonstrated his interest in the more profound aspects of life.

Interviewed by Eric Robson

Were you religious as a child?

I think my parents sent me to the Methodist Chapel because that was the way they'd been brought up and they thought that was the way I should be brought up. I used to go there in the way that one takes on a habit. Like going to school, it was part of the way of life. I don't think much of it really impinged upon me. I would recite these things rather in the way that my mother had — I really didn't comprehend much of it.

What image of God did you have in your Sunday School days?

A paternal, old man in the sky. I got a bit mixed up because one prayer was that all our doings should be ordered by 'thy governance' and I couldn't understand that word 'governance', I thought it was 'governess'. And I thought all our doings were ordered by a governess up there. Then I found out afterwards it wasn't governess it was governance: 'To do always that which is righteous in thy sight', that was the prayer.

In your early adult life, did you feel yourself drawn at all to a religious experience?

No, I don't think I did. I had a mass of form but no content. I knew about the way you went to church. What you had to listen to; the impact of a sermon. I knew what form it took and I was familiar with all that. But I had no real idea of the content at all — none of that occurred until the army.

When you were in the army in Ceylon, you had this moment – this revelation – which had a profound impact on your life.

Oh, an enormous impact: enormous. I was in a unit in Ceylon and we were housed in coconut matting huts in a coconut grove. The unit consisted of about thirty-five white men and the rest were all Indians. We were segregated as was the practice in the Far East, British Other Ranks Messes and the Indians were in Indian Other Ranks Messes. One day the Commanding Officer took all the men in lorries to go swimming. They all left the camp and I was duty NCO.

Was there a colonial atmosphere in this unit?

Oh, totally. The segregation was quite marked. You were not to mix with the other kind, you were to mix with your own and go into your own Messes and not into theirs. And they had a different kind of food from us. There was no mixing at all.

As I said, they all left and I was the only NCO on duty. I closed the office in the warmth of the afternoon, went to my bed and pulled the mosquito net down, put a towel round my middle because it was very hot and drifted off to sleep. I awoke to hear a terrible din and thought, 'What on earth is that?' I thought it must be a radio amplification and got up, tied the towel round my middle and went across to the Mess from where the noise was coming.

It was our radio being played and I thought, 'How can it be: all the white people have gone swimming?' I walked into the Mess and found it was full of Indians, Indian Other Ranks. They were all over the place; at tables, squatting on the floor; hundreds of them all round our radio which wasn't even War Office property. We'd all contributed, each sergeant of the unit and all the privates had contributed to buy it, for their own Mess. I walked in, switched off the radio and said, 'Get out! All of you, get out! You've no right to be in here, this is a British Other Ranks Mess, go to your own Mess and if you want to play a radio there, do so, but don't do it in here — get out!'

They all rose, very resentfully. They seemed to come towards me, with menace. Then a man rose from the ranks and I realised he was an officer. He told the men — in

Urdu — to leave; they came towards me and looked very closely at me. I felt a bit naked dressed only with a towel round my middle. They left and I went back to bed thinking I'd done the right thing.

Later on, I was wakened by somebody pushing at the mosquito net and jogging my elbow. It was the Commanding Officer. They'd returned from the swimming expedition and the C.O. said, 'What on earth's going on? I've heard the most appalling tale of grievances from all the Indians. Apparently you threw them all out.' I said, 'Yes, they'd no right to be in our Mess. It's a British Mess, they'd no right to be in there.' He said, 'They were all round that radio listening to a broadcast from Delhi about the imminent independence of India; we're treading very warily at the moment on a minefield because race relations are at a very critical stage. This is about a country achieving nationhood and the announcement they were listening to is going to affect all of them. It's hung about with a lot of problems. The Muslim problem and the Hindu problem. In the evacuation of certain territories, there is going to be a lot of trouble. This is why they were listening; it is something of enormous moment for them and you disrupted it. They're very angry. Apparently, you just said to their officer, 'Get out!' You didn't even give him his title. He's a Subara. You should have said, 'Subara Sahib!'

I said I was sorry and asked what I should do. He said, 'I think you should apologise. Just go over and say you're sorry.' I put on my shorts and he said, 'Not like that, in uniform, with puttees and blanker, the belt, the lot. You've got to do it: you insulted him in front of his men so you must apologise in front of his men.' The barrack room had filled up by then, with soldiers returning from swimming. They were saying, 'You're in it now Willie. You've really put yourself right in it, haven't you?' I was full of fear. The Commanding Officer said to me, 'Now rehearse this speech because when you march onto that field, you'll have to say the right things.'

I rehearsed it, got it off pat and walked on. I was fearful and feeling humiliated. They were all standing there watching somebody who hitherto had been quite arrogant, having to eat humble pie. I marched on and I did it. I saluted, 'Subara Sahib, I've behaved very wrongly. I failed to give you the respect that was due to your rank. I spoke in the heat of the moment. I hope very much you will be able to erase this appalling episode from your memory and accept my very sincere apologies.'

I saluted, thinking he would salute back and I would be given the order to march off. Instead of which he actually embraced me, put his arms round me, kissed both cheeks and said, 'You have spoken well, come and eat with us.' All his men cheered and they took me into their Mess and I sat and ate with them. During the meal I said, 'I honestly didn't expect this. I thought after I'd made a formal apology you would formally accept it; you would salute in return and I would march off.' He said, 'Oh, no. It's in your book, isn't it? "*Forgive us our trespasses, as we forgive them that trespass against us.*"'

I was thunderstruck and transfixed. It was a revelation for me because I'd said this a hundred times without any real concept of the import of the words. Suddenly I was being made aware of the real significance of the Lord's Prayer: not by somebody of my own race or creed but by some foreigner who didn't even speak my language. It came as a bolt from the blue because it made me start to look again at the entire prayer and the real meaning of 'Our Father which art in Heaven, *hallowed* be thy name, *Thy* kingdom come, *Thy will* be done on earth', instead of reciting it by rote with no real meaning for me at all.

Was this an immediate reaction?

What was immediate was the line, 'Forgive us our trespasses'. Suddenly I was aware of what trespass meant — to go onto territory and wound and hurt somebody — like going over a barbed wire fence. That is the true meaning of trespass. To wound, to inflict grave damage on somebody else's feelings. And that is what I'd done and I'd been forgiven for that. Suddenly being made aware of what that prayer really meant, made me examine just that bit of it. Later I started investigating the whole thing that I'd hitherto just trotted out, just as I trotted out 'goodbye', without understanding what it meant, 'God be with you'. The reason why our forefathers said it was that, if they couldn't be with you any more and they wanted someone to look after you, they trusted that He — because He was always there — would look after you.

We were talking earlier about your childhood experience of a contact with God, the paternalistic God. Many of the people speaking in this series have felt that their revelation brought them closer to God, did you have a similar feeling?

Immediately I started re-examining it, I started to realise how valuable it was. I think all my learning is bound up with what the words really mean. So often I'd been trotting out words without any real knowledge of what they meant. I had the form but not the content, and once I'd put the content back, the whole meaning of it fell into place. And the meaning of my faith fell into place. I realised it was nothing to do with scientific analysis, nothing to do with materialistic concepts; it's everything to do with the poetic interpretation of human life. We are created by an influence outside of ourselves; we enter this world with certain precepts, engraved if you like, upon our hearts, without ever knowing who put them there. But we are all of us, fundamentally aware of that outside influence on our lives,

and I would call that outside influence divine because there
is no materialistic explanation for it.

It's rather like the concept of nobility: a man diving into
the water to save the child. He may not even know the child
but he does it. Why does he do it? What instinct is he
obeying? How could you, materialistically, explain why
this noble thing moves us when it occurs and we say, 'Oh,
that was wonderful!' It does move us and it makes us feel
better for having known it.

*I've seen you quoted as saying that you consider yourself to be a
Christian, but you are not quite sure what sort of Christian. Does
this mean that revelation didn't give you all the answers but set
you off on a quest?*

I think that's what faith is about. It's all about a quest. He
gives us this insight into values outside ourselves, like truth,
goodness and beauty. We can't make the truth ourselves. It
exists outside of us but we might get a glimpse of it. He
created us and gave us self-will and the whole purpose of it
is what science can never explain. Science can give you
knowledge of how electricity is harnessed, how lightening
occurs but it can't tell you 'why'. What faith supplies is the
'why'. To realise the whole, to come to values like truth and
goodness and beauty, albeit in a minute way, is the desire, in
faith, to attain perfection and to see Our Lord as being the
perfect example of this.

*So how much of a practical influence has the memory of that
revelation had on the rest of your life and the way your career has
developed?*

Oh, enormous. My insight into the content was given to me
by a foreigner, someone of another colour, another skin. In
that moment, I realised that was quite deliberate: someone,
an alien, was chosen to enlighten me and it taught me above
all else, the nonsense of 'Europeans Only', colour of skin, all

the rest of it. It is nothing, just rubbish. I mean the outward signs, the masks, if you like, are nothing to do with fundamentals which are the human affections: that is what should concern us. Communicating with human affections is achieved through love which is why Auden's line, 'Love each other or die', is so potent.

Do you believe there is a mystical content in comedy?

Yes. A mysterious thing happens in an auditorium when laughter is created. An electric current seems to go through the whole auditorium and when it works, it works on a basis of mutual trust. The audience decide, 'we like you and we're going to accept what you are doing.' A tightrope is stretched out for an artist — on the one hand humility and on the other arrogance: 'I'm good enough to come on this stage, look I'm very good!' — and if it is kept tight enough, you walk on it and have everything under control. Sometimes I've gone along such a tightrope and teetered, come to near disaster, but I've never really worried because I'm quite certain there is a safety net. The hand of God is stretched below and will save me; I'll be caught.

Comedy is about the pricking of the bubble of pomposity which is a good thing because you are enlightened in the process.

You have mentioned the importance of love and yet, looking at some of your humour, it seems to be very spiteful. Isn't there a conflict between the two?

No. For instance, the rich lady getting out of the Rolls Royce with the poodle wearing the diamond collar and the old woman hobbling up with newspaper wrapped round her feet, saying, 'Lady, help me, I haven't eaten for three days,' and the rich woman replying, 'Well, my dear, you must simply force yourself!'

It's horrid in a certain interpretation: you can say, 'It's

appalling, a dreadful joke.' On the other hand, you could say it is funny because it's grotesque — you're taking an apparently incongruous comparison of two things which throws humanity into relief.

Does the divine contact that came to you during your revelation, help you to come to terms with despair?

It helps me to come to terms with despair by saying, be creative with it. If something is misery-making, talk about it, make it amusing, make it creative. That can be done with comedy. You can make it constructive. Happiness is an ephemeral thing and the most we can hope to achieve is a contentment with our lot. In accepting the vicissitudes and all the problems that are to be, but with the knowledge of all that you have achieved, you are compensating, keeping a balance and this way, I think, will achieve a certain amount of contentment.

Kenneth Williams, thank you very much.

EPILOGUE

The television series *Revelations* produced some fascinating correspondence. It was evident that many others had had similar experiences. The most striking feature of the letters was their sincerity: the writers were convinced that they had experienced something beyond the ordinary and yet quite real. Here, despite the dilemmas and confusions of everyday life, was something which could always be relied upon. Some letters speak of a sudden appreciation of beauty or love, some of a new understanding of events and existence and yet others of an immediate knowledge of appropriate action.

The findings of the Alister Hardy Research Centre at Oxford, endorse this. They have examined over four thousand experiences and are keen to receive more. In a recent publication they speak of significant links between direct religious experience and such factors as personal happiness, meaningfulness of life, lack of materialism and high levels of social responsibility. They suggest that most people associate the experience with a spiritual awareness.

In whatever way revelation is experienced it seems to be largely ignored by church and science. One of the saddest and most frequent comments of our correspondents was that there was nobody they could talk to about these moments; those who were in a position to give guidance were unable to help, understand or explain. People were frightened that the revelation and the inner certainty which so often accompanies it, would be regarded as strange, subjective, paranormal or even arrogant by others who may not have had a similar experience. Yet the Alister Hardy group have found that over sixty percent of people can recall an experience of a direct spiritual nature which has led them to the certainty that they have within them a greater world than ordinary senses, perceptions and thinking indicate.

All this suggests that spiritual understanding is not made

by our ordinary perception alone, no matter how objective we may try to be. And it appears to be personal, that is, proper and appropriate to each who experience it, whilst generous and outgoing as the contributors describe in this book.

Of course it would be dangerous to suggest that these moments of revelation are the only way to spiritual understanding. Faith, Action and Knowledge are traditionally held to be equal ways to Salvation. Nor would it be correct to suggest that revelation illuminates some exclusive Truth which is denied to the rest of us. But as so many of the contributors to this book have said, the experience is like a signpost or beacon which points the way and indicates the existence of a spiritual domain which can be trusted. And who would deny the need of this knowledge in today's society?

Ronald S. Lello
March 1985